L.A. COP

PEACEMAKER IN BLUE

BOB VERNON

ISBN: 978-1-63664-000-6

Printed in Korea
24 23 22 21 20 / 1 2 3 4 5

DEDICATION

To Esther, My Wife And Dearest Friend

FOREWORD

By John MacArthur
Pastor of Grace Community Church in Sun Valley, California
Chancellor of The Master's University and Seminary
President of Grace to You

I have always had great respect and admiration for those who are leaders, especially in the military and law enforcement. Life and death decisions are routine in the nature of the work when it is essentially defined as protecting people from dangerous evil. Bad decisions have detrimental impact and can be fatal. The reality is that the most critical decision-making is in the face of imminent danger. There are many who can lead in settings that do not have the threat of injury, but far fewer who can lead effectively while in the immediate presence of danger.

History shows that Bob Vernon was a leader and decision-maker who had such trust and respect from those who followed him that he ascended the ranks in a renowned meritocracy, to the highest level. That in itself would be enough accomplishment to earn honor and appreciation, but with Vernon there was much more—a transcendent leadership influence as a Christian. He exhibited this valuable dynamic in his life and in his effective communication of the gospel and the truth of Scripture. He applied the Bible and his experience to every aspect of his life. He was really a combination of cop and preacher.

I had the opportunity many times to be with him at camps and conferences, often preaching on the same platform. Through the years of fellowship and mutual ministry we developed a friendship that has enriched my life. Bob and Esther have become very dear to Patricia and myself. After his retirement he traveled the globe training police department leaders and giving his testimony to the gospel of the Lord he served. It is not likely that any police officer has had such a wide and effective ministry combining leadership principles with the message of the Word of God.

I am grateful to support bringing Bob Vernon's story to a new generation. Though no body cams were available during Bob's era, the stories he tells of the threats and triumphs of police work will put you in the middle of the action. In this video-saturated era, words can be worth a thousand pictures—enjoy the adventure.

John MacArthur

1

HOW DO YOU SAY DEAD?

"11L75, 11L75. Meet the fire department, 695 Maniton, possible D.B."

"Roger."

I wrote the address on the scratch pad secured to my metal log-sheet holder. After the address, I wrote "D.B.," police jargon for *dead body*. As I said the words to myself, they sounded as morbid as the first time I had heard them.

The radio call had interrupted the quietness of Sunday morning patrol. The streets were deserted except for an occasional well-washed family driving to an early religious service.

Only a few moments before I had been complaining to myself about working the Sunday day watch. I missed going to church with my family. Sunday calls, especially the morning ones, were always depressing. Usually it was family disputes; husbands and wives fighting about the happenings at a party the night before, or what to watch on TV.

I spun a U-turn in my black-and-white radio car and headed to Maniton. A few blocks and several turns later I saw a fireman disconnecting hoses from a hydrant. I pointed to the hoses ahead of me; he motioned me on. Down the street stood the smoldering frame of a house; a total loss. Although the walls were still standing, they would be leveled by wreckers. A hose from a pumper truck was still in use.

Across the street, a score of neighbors were clumped together. Some wore robes, others in pajamas huddled in blankets to keep out the morning chill. Two helmeted firemen with oxygen tanks on their backs were draping blankets around two young children standing next to the battalion chief's red car. Another fireman held a baby in his arms.

The scene was oppressively quiet. Grim. No one was smiling. In fact, no one was even talking. The only sounds were an occasional hissing as the spray from the nozzle of one of the mopping-up hoses hit live coals. As I stepped out of my car, a tall fireman with silver trumpets on his collar walked toward me. I supposed he was the chief.

"Morning," he said politely. "I'm afraid we have a D.B. in the front bedroom. We haven't disturbed anything in there except to spray in some water to knock down the fire. A couple of the men saw the body from the living room. I'm afraid it's the kids' mother."

"Only one body?" I asked.

"That's all we've seen so far."

"Well, let's have a look," I said. We walked toward the house. The chief continued, "She evidently thought one of the kids was still in there and went back in, but all three of them got out."

"Are there witnesses to her running in and not coming out?"

"Yeah, several in fact. We've detained them over by the pumper."

We walked through the safer portions of the smoldering shell. The smell of scorched furniture, wet rugs, and burnt paint stung my nostrils. We crossed what was once the living room and stopped at the doorway.

"You can see her from here," the chief said. He pointed through the purple haze to a steel-frame bed. On the blackened mattress was a form that reminded me of farm animal carcasses in barn and stable fires. The legs were bent sharply at the knees. The skin stretched tight, blackened and split in some areas. Her hair was gone.

"I've seen enough for now, chief. I'll call for the detectives and coroner. Don't let anyone in the room." Then the odor of burned flesh hit me and I backed away.

"Your first burn D.B.?" the chief asked.

"Yeah. Not a very pretty sight, huh?"

"No. She didn't feel much, though. She probably passed out from a lack of oxygen, or she inhaled super-heated air. From that point on, she didn't know what was happening."

"Maybe so, but it's still a bad way to go."

As we made our way across the front yard, I asked, "Do you have any idea how the fire started?"

"Yes, it's almost certain that someone threw a baby blanket over an open gas heater in the front room, probably to dry it out. It caught fire and spread to the curtains. Then the whole house went up."

"It doesn't sound like arson?"

"No, not at all. A paperboy saw the smoke and roused the people next door. They said that when they arrived, the occupants were asleep and the door was locked from the inside. But I've called the arson squad out anyhow."

I went to the squad car and radioed for detectives and the coroner. Now my job was only to preserve the scene and try to identify as many witnesses as possible. I had another task I was quite reluctant to tackle; it was my duty to make certain the children had someone to stay with.

I walked toward the three children. The older ones were sitting on the back seat of the chief's car and the fireman still held the little one. As I came up, he said in a low voice, "The kids want to know where their mommy is."

"They don't know yet?" I said, praying to myself that somebody had already told them.

"No, but I think the oldest suspects the worst. He wants to cry."

"Well, who's going to tell them?"

"That's up to you. They're yours. The neighbors say the father left over a year ago. They're not sure about any other relatives."

"Do you have their correct names and all the technical stuff?"

He pushed his helmet back on his head and wiped his forehead with a handkerchief. The eyes of the little one followed his motions with a suggestion of curiosity. "I think the oldest can give you the names all right. Any more than that, I'm afraid you'll have to work up."

I stood in the middle of the street feeling pretty helpless. Three children were in *my* care, their mother burned beyond recognition on a bed a few yards away. Sooner or later, they would have to know, and I was the one who would have to tell them.

I walked toward the car. What could I say? The little girl, no more than three, had her face pressed against the rear window, watching me. The boy, maybe five, had accepted the baby from the fireman and was holding his youngest sibling on his lap.

The little girl retreated to her brother's side when I opened the door. Her eyes reflected uncertainty. She wasn't sure about my uniform. I took off my hat and squatted down beside the open door.

"Hi, I'm Officer Vernon. I'm a policeman. I'm your friend." There was no verbal response, just those big eyes looking at me.

"What's your name?" I asked, placing a hand on the boy's knee.

"Rudy."

"How old are you, Rudy?"

"I'm almost five. I'm going to school next year."

"Rudy, will you please help me? Let's take your sister and the baby to my car, where it's warm. You can listen to my police radio."

"Okay, but where's my mom? Is she in the house?" Before I could answer, he shot me another question. "Did she get hurt in the house?"

His brown eyes connected with mine. He knew that his mother had met trouble.

"Yes, Rudy. Your mom has been hurt, but let's talk about that later, okay? Right now I need your help. You're the oldest, aren't you? Will you help me?"

"Yep, if you'll help my mom."

I nodded.

He pulled the blanket closer around the baby girl and started climbing out of the car.

"Here, I'll carry the baby. You bring your other sister." I held out my arms and he gently transferred the little one.

"Come on, Lupe," he said, grabbing the older sister's hands. "The policeman is our friend. He's going to help us ... You will help us, won't you?"

"Yes, I sure will."

We walked toward the squad car. The neighbors silently watched us; a policeman awkwardly carrying a baby in his arms, a baby who would grow up never remembering their mother, a small boy holding the policeman's hand on one side and his little sister on the other. A little boy in the crowd called out, "Hey, Rudy, where…" The boy's mother grabbed his arm and pulled him. He had no idea what he had done wrong.

I opened the door to the police car and watched Lupe scramble in. She was so young, so innocent, so trusting. To her, the police car looked like fun. But before Rudy got in, I stooped down next to him. "Look, Rudy, you can't stay in your house any longer. The fire ruined it. I'm going to take you to a nice place where they'll give you breakfast and let you play. But Lupe would get scared if she saw you cry. Then she might not want to go. So, you be big and brave, okay?"

I still hadn't found a good way to tell him about his mother. *Should I?* He was so young, so anxious. He looked back at the house. I knew he was concerned about his mother. "We won't leave her in there," I promised. "She's hurt so bad, some nice people will come and take her in another car."

He climbed onto the rear seat. As I handed him the baby, he looked straight into my eyes and asked, "Is my mommy dead?"

I was stunned. I'd figured he might not even understand the meaning of the word.

"Yes, Rudy, she's dead."

He snapped his head sideways and with his arms squeezed his baby sister as tight as he could.

The coroner and the detectives arrived, and I left with my three young charges. I drove them over to Lathrop Hall, where they would be well cared for. The juvenile people would probably place them in a foster home. I sat down at a desk there and finished the reports.

Well, it's all wrapped up, I said to myself. But, of course, it wasn't all wrapped up. It never is. Before I left, I went and said goodbye to Rudy. I left him standing in the hall, following me with his eyes. I was his friend, yet I had left him with strangers. When I went out the hall door, I could see him still watching me.

I wanted to take him in my arms and say, "Rudy, everything's going to be all right." But police work had brought me face to face with a harsh world that was completely foreign to the secure, happy world that I had known when I was Rudy's age. Somehow, I wasn't sure that everything was going to be all right.

I crawled into the car and radioed in. Before I could pull away, the operator came back on with a call. An older couple had been burglarized during the night and had just discovered it.

I rogered the call and entered the address on the log sheet. I checked the mirror, let out the clutch and moved into the traffic that was now heavy with Sunday morning worshippers returning home.

I wanted to tell those church people about Rudy, Lupe, and their baby sister, along with their young mother who had apparently died trying to see that her children were safe. As I sat alone in that car, I wanted to make some connection between the comfort and safety I had known in church and the stark reality of orphans and burned bodies.

As I hurried to the next call, I shot up a prayer for those three little kids without a mother or father. That was not the first prayer I had prayed while on the job amidst the conflicts I encountered as a peacemaker in blue. I knew the God who had guided me could take care of Rudy, Lupe, and their baby sister too.

2

A SEARCH FOR DESTINY

You see some scenes in life that you can never forget. It's as if we have a mental projector that can instantly flash memories across our minds, like that first D.B. call did for me.

There are other pictures in my life that are very vivid as well. Through my adolescent years I went to a number of summer camps. The one that impressed me the most was at Hume Lake. I was already a Christian between junior high and high school when I went to that camp. Until that time, however, I had never completely committed my life to Christ.

They had a very impressive service on closing night. We all went down to the lake. Those who wanted to make a statement about their relationship to God would be given a small paper plate and a candle.

I remembered stepping forward and taking the two items. For the first time I was very open and public about my relationship with God. I made a statement of commitment. I wanted God to do with me whatever He wanted to do. I lit my candle and put the plate on the lake.

I will always remember that night. It was an unforgettable sight for me. This act symbolized to each of us that we were putting our lives into God's hands for Him to direct.

As I left that camp and entered high school, I was continually thinking of what God would have in store for me. Unfortunately, I had the impression that in some mysterious way He would let me know His will. I kept expecting some revelation, but it didn't occur. In a way I was disappointed.

One night I came home from a date and walked past my dad's bedroom. He was up late as always. He invited me in to sit on the edge of his bed and visit with him. We had hundreds of talks like that as I was growing up. He asked if I had decided about college or not. We talked about the finances. He let me know that he couldn't do too much, but that he'd do everything he could to support me.

Dad didn't want me thinking about going to USC because it would cost too much. He asked if I had thought about Biola College. That really shocked me. My dad had recently become a Christian and as yet didn't show many of the expected indications of that decision. He attended church irregularly and never really became involved in its activities. Why would he suggest a Christian school?

About two weeks after the conversation with my dad, my sister, who was attending Biola, came home for a visit. Since she really liked the college, she encouraged me to go there for at least two years. Biola would give me a good foundation in the Bible.

One Sunday after church I was going through the line to shake hands with the pastor. I mentioned to him that I was interested in the Lord's will for my life and that I was praying about what college to attend. He said, "Biola."

I began to wonder if God could lead you in this way, instead of speaking in some miraculous way. Could He talk to you through your parents, your sister, your pastor? The final influence came when a friend of mine told me he was riding to Biola on his motorcycle. He offered to take me with him. By living at home and commuting we could cut down on the cost of going to college. I finally got the message that God was directing me to Biola. I applied and was accepted.

Another life-changing event took place during my two and a half years at Biola. It happened at a church social event held at the Moonlight Rollerway. There I met Esther, a hazel-eyed beauty who immediately caught my eye. By the end of the night, I was successful in getting her phone number. One date led to another and we soon discovered that we shared the same desire of finding God's direction in our lives. After a year of dating, I knew she was exactly what I was looking for and I decided to ask her to marry me. She said, "Yes!" From then on she was my closest prayer partner and together we sought God's will for our lives.

The Korean War was in progress, but during the first two years I had a deferment. The third year I did not, and I was reclassified 1A. I didn't want to be a foot soldier. I wanted to be a flier.

I had attended one of the two high schools in the United States that had classes in aeronautics. As a boy, I had loved everything connected with airplanes. I could identify each plane that flew over by its silhouette. My room was filled with model airplanes. The walls were plastered with pictures of planes, most of them given to me by an uncle who was an executive with Lockheed.

The greatest influence was the testimony of Grady Parrott who founded Missionary Aviation Fellowship. He had visited with me and described his experiences on the mission field. As a result of his encouragement, I had decided to let Uncle Sam teach me to fly so that later I could use those skills as a missionary aviation pilot.

Between semesters at Biola, I took preliminary cadet screening tests at Long Beach. I passed and was sent to Parks Air Base in Central California for a final week of testing. There were thirty of us. We spent the entire first day on a written examination. Next we took psychomotor tests to determine our mental-physical coordination. After each series of tests, our ranks decreased.

The next-to-last day was devoted to physical examinations, orientation, and propaganda movies. There were only five of us left now. They took us out on a parade field where we watched three Starfire jets perform. We were really revved up. There was only one exam left, a psychiatric exam. I was tired, but I wasn't worried. I had come this far with flying colors and I had no reason to consider myself anything but normal and well-adjusted.

I was assigned to a young psychiatrist. As soon as I sat down, he zeroed in on Biola.

"I see you went to a Bible school."

"Yes, but they teach more than the Bible."

"What religion are you?"

"I'm a Christian."

"You're a Christian, huh? You really believe there's a God. Next, you'll tell me Jesus was the Son of God?"

"Yes, sir."

I had never had a psychiatric examination before, but I surely hadn't expected this. What did his questions have to do with my application to be an aviation cadet? I was confused but didn't hesitate to state my beliefs.

"Do you believe Jesus was born without an earthly father—all that stuff?"

"Yes, I do."

"Let me see your fingernails."

Puzzled, I showed him my nails.

"Do you bite them?"

"No."

"Hm. There's quite a bit of moisture in your palms. Do you stammer or stutter?"

"No."

"Did you stutter when you were younger?"

I shook my head.

"Did you wet the bed when you were little?"

"Not often, so far as I know."

He looked at my medical history. "I see your father has stomach trouble."

"That's right."

"Well, it all fits together. Although we have neither the time nor the inclination to do a psychological profile on your family, I see evidence of a great deal of emotional instability. Your hyper-religiousness is a strong sign. We certainly don't need people like you in Korea. At the first sign of danger, you'd flee back to the base to pray to your Heavenly Father to keep you safe from harm. I'm going to have to disqualify you."

On the basis of a three-minute conversation, he was ruling me out. There had been no substance to his examination, just my faith, my fingernails, and my dad's stomach. I had heard that the psychiatrists sometimes baited you to see if you would blow up. Maybe he was assaulting my religious beliefs to see if I could take it. So I just sat there.

He looked up, irritated. "Go ahead. I'm through with you."

I said, 'Thank you, sir." I stood and started walking out slowly. *He'll call me back. It's all part of the test.*

Once outside, I realized it was over. I couldn't believe it. I had survived a week of testing; now, three minutes of dumb questions and I was out. Up until now, everything had seemed so right.

Dismayed, I went to see the head of the selection team. While waiting to see him, I explained my plight to his aide. As I was telling my story, the colonel got out of his chair and came over. "Was that Lieutenant Smitherson?"

"Yes, sir. How did you know?"

"Well, you're not the first."

He conferred with his adjutant, then said to me, "Look, I'm a colonel and he's only a lieutenant, but he's a specialist and I can't overrule him. In my opinion, though, you have a good basis for a protest. Here's the address to write in Washington. You may win an examination by a panel of two or three psychiatrists, and if they decide you're okay, they will overrule the lieutenant. Knowing his other tricks, it really sounds like you got a bad deal. I'm sorry."

I fully intended to follow through, to write to Washington, enter the cadet program and ultimately fly planes in Korea and then become a missionary pilot. I was positive that this was God's will. Yet why had this happened to me? On the plane to Los Angeles the impact of flunking out hit me. I had been condemned because of my faith in God. Of all the psychiatrists on the base, I had gotten one who was opposed to personal religious faith.

I tried to console myself. I told myself it was for the best. I honestly wanted to be obedient to God's will for my life. Perhaps my failure was God's way of intervening. Still, I came back home really depressed.

Things continued going downhill for me. It was already too late to register for the next semester at Biola. Within days, I received a notice to take my physical for induction. I passed it and was told I would be drafted within thirty to sixty days. It seemed I was destined to be a foot soldier after all.

Thirty days went by, then sixty days and no draft call came. *Had the draft board decided they didn't want me?* I was idle and wondered what I should do. One day, while discussing my situation with my dad, he said, "Son, I know you've always been interested in police work. Why don't you consider taking the test for the L.A.P.D. Academy next week?"

I thought about it. Dad was right. I was interested in police work. My dad was a policeman and his work had always fascinated me. Still, I had qualms about such a career. I vaguely believed that being a policeman wasn't a Christian profession. There was so much violence associated with it. Still, I had no other leading. That night, I concluded that if the Lord didn't want me to be a cop, he would see to it that I flunked out, the same way I had flunked at Parks. Besides, I believed the draft would get me very soon.

I filed for the exam, which was only given every two years. Along with three thousand other candidates, I took the tests on a Saturday at Hollywood High School. The processes were similar to those at Parks, a written exam and then an oral exam.

My dad had coached me, and he told me that during the oral exam they would ask something to check my capacity for memory. "When I arrived at the department, they asked me to describe the secretary who had brought me into the room. I'll bet they ask you the same thing." I assured him I would be ready for that.

The board was composed of one sergeant and two prominent citizens, all in plainclothes. A secretary escorted me in for the interview and introduced me to each member of the panel. All the while, I kept my eyes on her, making mental note of every detail of her person, grooming, and dress.

They proceeded with questions to test my judgment, and I answered them fairly well. Then at the end of the interview, just as I had expected, one of the interviewers said, "Mr. Vernon, part of a policeman's job is testifying in court to things that he hears and sees. What do you think about your capacity for memory?"

"I have a good memory, sir." *Here it comes, and am I ready!*

"Very good. Then I'm sure you recall people's names?"

I had paid no attention whatsoever to their names. I couldn't remember one of them. I stumbled around, misnaming all of them. My face was flushed and I knew I had flunked out again. I had no option but to level. I'm sorry, but I really thought I had this test aced! My father is a policeman, and he said you would test my memory, except he said you would ask about the woman who brought me in here. That is what *he* was asked. I was ready for that one. I was concentrating so hard on her, I didn't pay attention to anything else that was going on."

They all laughed. I'm glad you told us," one of them said. "I thought it was strange the way you were eyeing her. All right, we don't want to disappoint you. Tell us about her."

I did, right down to the shade of her fingernail polish. They got a big laugh, and I received a very high score. Later, the sergeant told me that my confession saved me.

Next came a test for agility, followed by an obstacle course and a physical examination. Then came the psychiatric screening. I was uptight until I saw that it was based on more than the evaluation of one professional; it included the Minnesota Multiphasic Personality Inventory, the Rorschach Test, and others.

A few weeks later, when the tests had been evaluated and scored, I was called downtown for an interview. My appointment was with a consulting psychiatrist of the city of Los Angeles. The first thing he said was, "Mr. Vernon, your scores show that you were very apprehensive about the exam."

"That's right, I was."

"Why?"

"I would rather not talk about it."

"If you don't, I'll have to fail you."

I told him what happened at Parks Air Base.

"You mean you believe in a personal God?" he asked.

Oh, no! Here we go again! For a moment, I was tempted to play down my faith. Fortunately, I didn't. I thought, If God wants me to be an L.A. policeman, no shrink will be able to keep me out. And if God doesn't want me to be one, I don't want to be here anyway.

I decided to be totally honest and let the chips fall where they would. I answered the questions openly and fully; I even volunteered that I knew Jesus personally. *If this doesn't do it, nothing will.*

"You really believe all that?"

"Yes, sir, I really do."

His response caught me totally off guard. He said, "That's

great! I'm glad to see a young man who knows what he believes in. I was especially impressed when I tried to get you to back down and you wouldn't."

As I recovered, he went on. "Mr. Vernon, there are conflicting opinions in the psychiatric world about the value of religious beliefs. I come from a different school than the psychiatrist you dealt with at Parks. In fact, the services are already getting feedback from Korea indicating that in enemy prison camps our men who have religious faith are the strongest. As a result, the Communists are separating the religious ones from the others, lest their faith spreads. That leads me to believe that, in many instances, religious faith makes you more, not less stable."

Now I was anxious. Would I receive an appointment or was this another closed door?

Esther and I had been looking forward to getting married, but now, the future appeared uncertain. The possibility of being drafted lay heavily on my mind. Separation from Esther would be a factor. Newlywed friends enthusiastically urged us to "tie the knot" soon, assuring me that things would work out one way or the other. Esther and I took a leap of faith and set the wedding date!

3

MORE SWEAT, LESS BLOOD

Esther and I were married on September 17th, 1954. Just two weeks later, at 7 A.M. on October 1st I found myself standing on the volleyball court of the Los Angeles Police Academy with eighty-one other men who had passed the selection screening and had received appointments. To most of us, the academy was an unknown institution. Although as a boy I had spent many summer days around its Olympic-size pool, I didn't know what to expect that morning.

A policeman in blue asked us to fall in and form ranks according to height. After considerable shoving and stumbling, we accomplished that.

"How many of you have not had military experience?" he asked.

Only three of us responded. I had yet to learn how much of a disadvantage that would be. The training officer told us oddballs to watch what the rest did and try to follow.

"All right, you guys want to be police officers," he said. "Well, we're going to see how serious you are. You've made it through a selection process that less than five out of every hundred pass. That means you are qualified; you can make it if you want. But the training is tough, so tough that some of you won't be standing with the group at graduation."

I'll be there! I thought to myself confidently.

"We have a saying, 'The more you sweat here, the less you'll bleed on the streets.' It's our job to prepare you for the tests you'll meet on the streets, whether they be physical, mental, or emotional tests. We want you to be well-prepared."

"Those of you who make it *will* be prepared. You'll be a member of the finest police department in the world. You'll have skills, abilities, and confidence you never thought you could have. You'll act differently; you'll even look a little different than you look today. You'll be a Los Angeles policeman. That's one of the reasons we're going to take your picture this first day. That way, later you can see and appreciate the change."

He disappeared into the main complex of buildings. As we waited for him to return with the photographer, some of us commented that the red tile roofing and mission-style arches gave the facility a country club atmosphere rather than that of a police boot camp.

Soon the picture was taken and we were ushered into a classroom to fill out forms and be sworn in. During lunch in the academy restaurant, I learned that more than half the men came from southern California. The others had come from all over the nation. Several had law enforcement experience in other places. Because I was one of the three without military experience, I was anxious to learn from the others.

I remember a red-headed ex-marine, Taylor, saying, "Look, kid, you don't want any of the instructors to get to know you. Don't ask a lot of questions and don't volunteer for nothing. Just be bland. Not too sharp, not too dull. Kinda in the middle. Okay?"

A guy just out of airborne service chimed in. "Act like you know what's happening even if you don't. I knew a guy who beat the system with a clipboard. Every time an officer came around, this fellow picked up his clipboard and acted busy. If he was in the barracks and an officer came in, he started counting mattresses or something. He made it through the whole program with no sweat."

After lunch, the orientation continued. We were to get short haircuts and trim our fingernails so that no one would get scratched during self-defense training. Our G.I. shoes were to be spit-shined. We were to wear a clean uniform every day, pressed the night before with military creases in the shirts.

When wishing to address an instructor, I was to stand at attention and state in a loud voice, "Officer Jones, sir, recruit Vernon, sir." I was to remain at attention until the instructor recognized me. To me, all of this regimentation seemed stupid and unnecessary, but I would have to go along with it.

We were issued uniforms and equipment. Instead of badges, we were given plastic nameplates to wear on our shirts. The wearer of a plastic nameplate had to park on the street, below the academy parking lot. Later, we would be issued a permanent metal nameplate, which would permit parking in the lot. Late in the training program, an L.A.P.D. badge would be issued, according the wearer almost as much status as a regular officer. During the third week, we were issued revolvers.

During the first week of physical training I abruptly learned how much of a disadvantage my lack of military training was for me. Being one of the younger members of the class, I was in reasonably good shape. I had taught swimming and weight lifting at a boys' camp on Catalina Island during summers. On this particular day, an instructor was leading the push-ups and calling the cadence as he performed the exercise. He kept the pace rather slow to accommodate those who lacked conditioning, and I had no trouble keeping up.

Several instructors circulated to make sure our form was correct and to shout words of encouragement. The smell of Bermuda grass and dirt reminded me of football practice. Although the pace was slow, the reps were starting to get to me; it was getting a little harder to keep my body stiff and avoid a sagging stomach. I had gotten a bit sloppy when I became aware that an instructor was standing over me. I began pushing briskly up to full arm extension, holding the body stiff, and moving precisely to the cadence called. Maybe it bothered him to see me exercising too effortlessly. Whatever his reason, he barked, "Faster, Vernon, faster!"

His order didn't make sense. I was perfectly synchronized with the lead instructor, and I pointed that out to him. "I'm going as fast as everyone else."

He was incredulous. "What did you say?"

I sensed he was angry, but I couldn't figure why, so I repeated, "I'm going as fast as everyone else."

In the line ahead of me I saw Taylor, the ex-marine, shaking his head. Now the instructor was really mad. The blood vessels in his neck were sticking out. He shouted, "Give me ten laps. Ten laps, Vernon!"

"Now?"

"Right now, right now!" He pointed to the track. As I double-timed toward the track, I looked back and saw that my fellow cadets were intent on ignoring me; they didn't want to be my running mate. I grudgingly ran my laps.

In the locker room after my workout, I was smarting from having been punished when I hadn't done anything wrong. Still perspiring from the ordeal and drying off a second time after my shower, I was afraid the fifteen-minute period for changing would expire before I got dressed.

The corridors between lockers were crowded with recruits trying to dress. With no benches to sit on, several were leaning against the lockers, putting on their shoes when someone yelled,

"Make a hole!" That was another protocol. We had to snap to attention, no matter the state of dress or undress, and make room for the instructor to walk between the rows of lockers. This time it was Nichols, the one who had punished me with the laps. As he came down the aisle, his eyes met mine. He stopped and without a change of facial expression said, "Vernon, did you get the message?"

"Yes."

"Yes, *what?*" I could see he was getting angry again.

Then I remembered. "Yes, sir!"

He continued down the aisle, reminding us we had less than five minutes to finish dressing and report for weapons training. After he was out of earshot, a fellow whose locker was next to mine asked, "Aren't you one of the guys who hasn't been in the service?"

"Yeah."

"Look, you'll get along a lot better if you just do what they say. Don't try to figure out *why*, just do it. They're trying to train you to submit unquestioningly to authority."

"I was doing the push-ups as fast as everyone else. If I had gone faster, I would have been out of sync."

"That doesn't matter. What was important was he wanted you to go faster. Take my advice and do whatever they say."

During physical training the following day, we were doing push-ups and I saw Nichols coming my way. He stood beside me for a short time, then quietly but firmly said, "Vernon, faster."

I picked up the pace, almost doubling it. He watched. I guess I didn't tire fast enough, or perhaps he wanted to test my self-control when provoked; anyhow, he stepped closer and placed one of his feet on my back between my shoulder blades. The pressure slowed my pace. Soon I could hardly manage to come up. I was about to collapse when he spoke again, his voice louder, the pitch higher, "Vernon, do you really want to be a Los Angeles police officer?"

The question caused me to find a new reserve of energy.

"Yes." Then I remembered. "Yes, sir."

He took his foot off and continued down the ranks. That same individualized drill took place the next three days, apparently until he was satisfied that I could keep cool when provoked.

Others weren't so fortunate. One afternoon while we were running wind sprints, Burnside was loafing. Instructor Johnson ordered another recruit to get on Burnside's back. Then he ordered Burnside to run the wind sprints carrying the other man piggy-back. Halfway across the field Burnside stopped, shook off his passenger, and advanced on the instructor. "Nobody can treat me like this!" he screamed, unleashing a string of profanity.

By the time we hit the showers, Burnside's locker had already been cleaned out. I felt sorry for him, and at first I thought the pressure was unfair. But in the years since, time and again I have seen convincing evidence that a cop cannot succumb to emotional pressure, even if that pressure seems unreasonable or unwarranted.

The stress training and submission to authority were hard lessons for most of us to appreciate. But as the training progressed, we were exposed to more situations simulating the demanding conditions we would face in the field as "street cops." Day by day we developed more and more skills and insight.

We talked about police behavioral patterns, like the "pursuit syndrome." This takes place after you've chased some clown at speeds of up to ninety miles an hour through residential areas and across crowded intersections until you have finally caught him. Now your fear has turned to anger and it's boiling over. You feel an almost overwhelming urge to punish them then and there. Yet, through classroom and field training, we began to recognize reasons for keeping cool.

Many of us were "killed" by an instructor playing the role of a bandit. The instructor would fire a blank from his gun when we were careless during a vehicle pull-over or body search.

Gradually, the rigorous training began making sense.

Time was passing quickly. The days were full of deadlines, one after another.

"Double-time to the combat range for silhouette firing."

"Double-time to the field for parade drill."

"Go to your lockers, dress in fatigues for prone searching techniques, and be on the field in ten minutes."

"Double-time to classroom one for first aid instruction."

At night there was an impossible load of homework. I often studied law and criminal procedure while in a hot bath trying to soothe my aching muscles for the next day's calisthenics and self-defense throws.

Also, I had to prepare my uniform and clean my gun. My wife, Esther, still hates the smell of gun oil. It permeated our house during those months at the academy, which unfortunately coincided with her being pregnant. She still associates Hoppe's No. 9 nitro oil with morning sickness. Every night I had to run the copper wire brush and felt pads through the bore of my .38 Special. A six-inch barrel on the .44 frame made it easy to learn to shoot, but tedious to clean.

The discipline and order began to soak in and I started believing the rhetoric I heard every day: "This is the finest police organization in the world. If you graduate from this institution, there is no situation or person you will meet on the streets that you won't be able to handle."

The distance runs benefited me beyond just getting my body in shape. For months and years later, I would appreciate what some call the "hang-in-there" training. We came to realize we could do more than we thought we could. The six-mile run is the best example. I remember thinking, "I can't do it. This is too much!" Then an instructor would come alongside and needle me for slowing down. I would get so mad I would force myself to do it just to show him.

One of the most inspiring examples of what the six-mile run

can do happened to a cop named Rudy. Several years after completing his academy training, Rudy and his partner pulled over a car containing four men. It was a routine inspection. As the officers approached the car, one of the four men—all were Black Panthers—leaned out and began firing with an automatic pistol. Both officers were shot. Rudy was shot twice in the leg, one wound resulting in a compound fracture. He was also shot in the groin, the chest, and in both hands. The four Panthers piled out of the car and continued shooting, apparently intending to finish the officers off.

Afterwards Rudy said he was so badly hurt that he didn't think he had a chance to survive, much less fight back. But then an event flashed before him; the six-mile run at the academy. He remembered running it for the first time. As he started up the last hill he thought, *I can't make it.* But one of the instructors came alongside him, running backwards and taunting him. He thought, *if they can do it backwards, I can do it frontwards.*

That episode showed him that he was capable of doing things he didn't think he could do. So now, instead of giving up and being finished off, he managed to get himself into a sitting position and engaged the Panthers in a gunfight. His partner, who had also been hit, kept firing, too. When it was over, three Panthers lay dead and one was wounded.

So, there were good, solid reasons for what we were being taught, and one of them was survival. The "Officer Survival" and "When to Shoot" lectures were among the most sobering experiences. In each session, recent "officer-involved shooting" situations were discussed and critiqued. Clearly, shooting too soon or without a sufficient basis of necessary and legal cause could mean imprisonment; on the other hand, hesitation sometimes meant the death of an innocent citizen, the officer himself, or his partner.

Those sessions shook me. For some reason, I had never really given much thought to the possibility of being killed. My father had survived twenty years of police work. Moreover, our national mythology is that the "good guys" are rarely killed. Sometimes they are wounded, but almost always they survive.

Evidently, the instructors were aware of our misconception. To combat it, they passed around photos depicting L.A.P.D. officers who had been killed on duty. It took all the nerve I could muster to absorb the horror of those photographs of a policeman in full uniform lying on the pavement, a trickle of blood flowing from the side of his mouth, his open eyes reflecting his violent death. It was quite clear—police officers die. And, almost as sobering— sometimes they must kill.

One of the police killings that really got to me involved two cops in their twenties, Officers Scebbi and Espinoza. One night, they were patrolling a residential area and stopped to interrogate a man whose movements were suspicious. He was wearing sneakers which, at that time, triggered *burglary* in almost any officer's mind. When they got out of the car to talk to him, they had no idea that he had in his waistband under his shirt a small caliber revolver.

When the officers asked him what he was doing in the neighborhood, his answers seemed convincing. "Well, let's have some I.D.," one said. He gave them an identification card. One of the officers wedged his flashlight under his chin and began writing a field interview card. Then the guy went for his gun, completely surprising both officers. Instinctively, Scebbi dropped his flashlight and threw himself forward to give the guy a push. The man fired, hitting Scebbi in the stomach. He also shot Espinoza. The bullet struck his chin, knocking him down. The man turned and ran down the street.

Scebbi crawled over to the police car, managed to get his hand on the microphone, and reported, "Officer needs help." He gave the location. After that, the operator could hear only gurgling. Later, a doctor said Scebbi probably died within 25 seconds of being hit. The bullet had severed the aorta, the trunk artery.

Espinoza, although wounded in the jaw, fired his revolver at the fleeing man, striking one leg and breaking it. The man went down, turned, and fired back, hitting Espinoza in the stomach. Espinoza shouted for Scebbi. Getting no response, he dragged himself over to the car and found Scebbi lying in the seat, the microphone in his hand.

Within minutes, other units arrived. They discovered the killer hiding in a clump of bushes. Like in a movie melodrama, he started crying to the gathering bystanders, "Don't let them kill me! Don't let these cops kill me! Don't shoot me! I didn't mean to hurt anybody!"

They took a picture of Scebbi. I'll never forget it. The crisp uniform. The highly polished badge. The open eyes. The microphone clutched in his hand. When I saw it, I realized as never before, *you can die doing this job.* And you can also kill, or put a man in jail. Those are the two most important things a man possesses: life and freedom. A solemn responsibility.

Finally, the big day came; graduation. On January 23, 1955, seventy-three of us, out of a beginning class of eighty-one listened as Chief of Police, William H. Parker, issued a rousing challenge. He exhorted us to embrace integrity and pursue professionalism. With religious fervor, he spoke of the "thin blue line" that maintains the delicate balance between individual freedom and social order. As we marched behind the band and past the reviewing party, I thought, *This is it. I've made it. I'm an L.A. cop.*

Contrary to what I had thought would happen, I still hadn't been drafted. After I finished the academy, I became concerned as to why I had not been. I didn't want to go into military service, but I didn't want to shirk my duty either. I thought they must have lost my file. Finally, I drove over to Alhambra to my draft board's office.

"I was told I would be inducted in 60 days," I said to the clerk, "but that deadline passed months ago. I thought you might have lost my card. I don't want to be drafted, but I want to be fair."

She looked perplexed. She summoned her superior and he said, "I can't remember this ever happening before."

He located my file and studied it. "We have a notation you're an L.A. policeman. Is that correct?"

"Yes, sir."

"Well, that's the reason. Being a policeman doesn't reclassify you; you are still 1A, but it means we'll take everybody else in your category ahead of you. We will have to take you before we drop to the next classification, but not before. You're in a sensitive job. We don't like to rob communities of the essential services that you policemen deliver."

They never did get down below my category, and I never was drafted.

4

THE ROOKIE

My first assignment after graduating from the academy was Central Division. I was elated that I would be on patrol in the same division my father had worked. That beat offered diversity and an opportunity for plenty of work. It embraced Skid Row, East Fifth Street, the Main Street Bar, Grand Central Market, and the con men.

Best of all, Central Division still had foot patrols. In most other areas policemen on foot had been replaced by radio cars. They were generally regarded as low in status, but not to me. I could still recall some of those adventures that my dad had shared with me about his years as a flatfoot. He had impressed me with the way he answered the challenge of getting along with the people, gaining their confidence and respect (even winning the respect of known criminals), and getting people to provide the information needed to help him keep his turf clean.

Central Division was all I expected and more. The first couple of months, I "worked the field," or wherever they needed an extra body. I walked beats, rode the drunk wagons, and occasionally went out in a radio car. I even got a whirl with a plainclothes pickpocket detail.

The first time I was assigned to a pickpocket detail, I fancifully thought of myself as a detective! By department definition I wasn't, but working out of uniform was to me a show of status. I thought I was playing it cool standing at Seventh and Broadway watching the streetcar safety zone. I didn't know what to look for, but that wasn't my primary function, anyway. I was the "chase man." I was to run down any suspect that either of my two experienced partners detected and had attempted to arrest.

My partners had wisely placed me in a position back from the safety zone and somewhat screened from view. By blending in with pedestrian traffic I was feeling secure when a short, black man sauntered up. He grinned and asked, "Say, officer, do you have the time?"

"It's ten-fifteen."

Then it hit me. "Hey, how did you know I'm a cop?"

"Just checking you out, brother. Just checking you out." Laughing, he bopped down the sidewalk, turning two or three times to "shoot" at me with his extended index finger.

Each day brought new experiences. Even each drunk arrest presented a different twist. One day, I was walking Main Street with legendary Officer Bill Shirley when a trucker told us, "There's a wino in that alley. I nearly ran him over."

When we found him, I started to bend over and pull him up.

"Wait a minute, kid," Shirley cautioned. With his nightstick, he pushed the poor fellow's pants up on one side, exposing an ankle. Several lice scurried away.

"You don't want to take a bunch of these home with you," he said. He handed me his book of short-form arrest reports and said, "Fill out as much of this as you can and I'll go call a wagon."

Shirley signaled from a nearby call box, and in a few minutes we were loading the drunk into a "Black Moriah" drunk wagon. He would be taken to our main jail, along with several other drunks collected from beat officers and radio cars working the district. Part of his processing would include medical attention and a delousing shower.

Shirley said to the wagon driver, "Pull around the corner for a minute, will you? I think we have some more customers for you."

The wagon pulled against the curb in front of a newsstand. Shirley hopped up on the metal step at the rear and opened both doors. "Rhinegold Express now leaving for Lincoln Heights," he bellowed. "Clean shower, hot meals, and a dry bed. All aboard!"

To my amazement, several derelicts came staggering from two of the five bars within shouting distance and "surrendered." There was no coercion, let alone force. That was one thing I noticed about Shirley and other veterans—even when a belligerent and bull-strong arrestee didn't want to go, somehow they could persuade him into the slammer without a fight. They knew how to choose from psychology, humor, and physical persuasion.

The next day, I was assigned to a drunk wagon called "1B1." We would make hourly trips to the old Lincoln Heights jail, delivering persons we picked up from beat and radio car officers. On some runs, we accumulated up to a dozen people.

Early in the day, I became aware of a problem that plagued all "Black Moriah" officers. The passengers wanted to fight—not with us usually, but with one another. Since we were responsible for their safety and well-being, it was our duty to prevent or break up the fights.

On one of our jaunts, we had a full wagon and the last "customer" was trying to fight all of the rest. I was sitting with my swivel seat turned backward so that I could babysit.

"Hey, partner," I said. "Don't think I'm nuts, but I'm going to try something weird to keep these guys in a good mood."

"All right, Vernon. But if you're thinking of giving them some of *that,* don't." He pointed to a cardboard box of liquor bottles we had taken from our passengers. "I tried it once—thought I'd anesthetize 'em and the sergeant really got on my case."

"I wasn't thinking of that." I pushed back the sliding door to the prisoners' compartment. "Hey, you guys, how about a song for old times? Something you all know. How about 'Show Me The Way To Go Home?'"

The ones who hadn't drifted off into never-never-land turned toward me with quizzical looks. Then the fighter, who was sitting on top of another guy back at the rear door held up his hand and slurred, "Shweeet Addeliine."

I began to sing and the fighter and a couple of others joined in. As we drove up Spring Street and all the way to the jail, I repeatedly led the chorus of "Sweet Adeline." As we stopped at traffic signals, motorists would look around for the source of music—if you could call it that. They found it hard to believe that the glee club was behind the screened windows of a police van. At one stoplight, a man in a car beside us joined in for a couple of bars.

In spite of my success as a drunk wagon chorus leader, the assignment I really coveted was to work solo. I recognized that being young, inexperienced, and still in the six-month probationary period, the opportunity would probably be a long time coming. Still, somehow I kept hoping that when I checked the assignment board (which was posted at the end of each watch and told us where we would be working the following day), I would somehow luck into a solo situation.

One morning I reported for duty, expecting to work the Third Street foot beat with Sid Goldman, but I didn't find Sid in the locker room. I went into the roll call room and he wasn't there, either. I thought to myself, *perhaps he had a court case and would show up late.* But when the lieutenant read off the assignments, he explained that Sid had called in sick. I would be working the beat alone, he said.

I started feeling butterflies as one of the sergeants read off the daily "hot sheet" of stolen and wanted vehicles. I felt even more anxious, when after roll call and inspection, one of the sergeants said he wanted to see me in the watch commander's office.

I must have looked apprehensive, because as I left the inspection line to retrieve my citation and short-form arrest books, Officer Milhouse stopped me and said, "Vernon, I'm working 1XL48. My car will be in your area. I know how spooky it is to walk alone the first time. If you get nervous about something, give me a call."

I looked into his freckled face. He wasn't putting me on. "Thanks," I said. "If it gets too lonely out there, I'll give you a call and buy the coffee."

"You're on. Best offer I'll have all day." Then he added, "The watch commander's office is thataway."

I stood outside Sergeant Heinrich's office. Although I was uptight, I found it amusing to eavesdrop and watch his face turn red as he tried to explain to "Salty" why he couldn't have the next day off. Finally, despairing of logic, he blurted, "Michekay, you work tomorrow 'cause I've got three stripes and I say you work tomorrow. Right?"

"Okay, Sarge. Don't get mad. Nothing ventured, nothing gained, right?" As Salty walked past me, he rolled his eyes at the ceiling in an expression of frustration.

Sergeant Heinrich was a 30-year-plus veteran. His longevity was indicated by the eye-filling six hash marks sewn on his left forearm below the sergeant stripes. You could barely see the police midnight blue with all those white stripes. He looked up at me and paused, trying to recall why he had asked me in. Then, remembering, he reached into his left top drawer. He talked as he leafed through papers. "Look, Vernon. You're a big kid and can handle yourself awright. I'm kinda short on deployment today, so I'm going to let you walk alone. Stay out of trouble, and if you need help or advice, be humble enough to call, okay?"

"Yes, sir."

"Now there's something else I wanted to tell you, if I can find the paperwork. Here it is. Now listen. The detectives want this guy pretty bad. There are two felony warrants on him. He's an escapee from the joint; likely armed, probably dangerous. We've had reports he's hanging around your beat. Remember this—he said he won't be taken alive."

With more bravado than anything I said, "Okay, how shall I handle it?"

"Go over to Records and Identification and pick up his mug. If you spot him, get some help."

At R and I, I picked up the photo and stood for a minute looking at it. He looked like a bad actor, but most of them did. I started to put the photo in a pocket, but remembered that I didn't want to pull the picture out every time I checked someone out. So I took off my hat and slid the picture beneath the clear plastic lining. I caught a bus and a few blocks away, jumped off on my beat.

As·I walked the streets that day, I was a picture of exaggerated politeness. When I approached anyone faintly resembling the fellow in the photo, I doffed my cap and said, "Hello, sir," stealing a quick peek at the mug-shot.

The day passed fairly uneventfully. I booked a couple of drunks, broke up a fight in the Fig Leaf Cafe, and talked to several businessmen about security problems. I also had them look at the picture. An auctioneer recognized him. "Yep, I've seen him around a couple of the bars."

Late that afternoon I walked into Bert's Bar, in the Second and Figueroa area. When my eyes adjusted to the dark, I saw my man! He was at the end of the bar. I didn't see how I could be mistaken; I'd been looking at that mug all day. Now the search had ended. There he was! I thought about finding a telephone and calling for help, but decided he might leave before help came. I had to grab him by myself.

I eased toward him. He didn't see me, but the bartender and the patron did, and they shied away, like in the old gunfighter movies. That didn't help my confidence. Suddenly, all the training I had received in the police academy simply left me. I did a dumb thing. I walked up right behind him and took off my cap. I reached around and shoved the cap and the photo right in his face. "Mister, is this you?" I demanded.

He was an experienced thug, but understandably he had never seen his mug in a cop's hat before. He was so surprised, he turned around and said, "Yep, that's me."

I had my hand on my gun, which was in a clamshell holster that snapped open when a concealed button was pressed. This fellow was savvy, so when I hit the button he wasn't surprised to find himself staring at my .38 revolver. What did startle and frighten him was the way the gun was wavering. I was scared and he knew it.

"Take it easy, officer. Don't get excited. Don't shoot. What do you want me to do?"

Getting rid of my hat by tossing it on the counter, I reached down and pulled my handcuffs from my Sam Browne belt. "Here, I want you to put these on," I instructed.

He was so relieved not to have his head blown off, he actually helped me get the cuffs on his wrists.

When we got to the station, the watch commander asked my prisoner, "What happened? You put the word out that you wouldn't be taken alive. Yet, the officer here says you didn't even go for your gun."

"Sarge, one look at the kid's face and at that gun swinging around convinced me that any move and it was certain death."

Working with experienced cops like Bill Shirley proved to be more valuable training than my solo ventures. Bill and I were walking the South Main Street beat. A young man coming out of a girlie-flick turned abruptly upon seeing us and went back into the theater. We figured he should be checked out. When we pulled out his I.D., a phony police badge fell onto the floor. Later, at the station, we discovered he was an illegal alien and had pulled six street robberies in the last two weeks. He used the badge to impersonate a vice officer. During his searches, he robbed his victims.

A policeman is trained to feel a sense of achievement when he stops any source of crime. It is an especially good feeling to arrest impersonators who have been using badges to commit crime. Stories about cops-turned-bad make every officer suffer. It doesn't matter that there are thousands of honest cops. Any time there is bad news, you can count on being hit in the face with insults and innuendos. You stop someone for a traffic violation and while you're completing the citation, they taunt, "Are you one of those cops who got caught last week burglarizing that nursery in West Los Angeles?" What do you say? Nobody hates a bad cop, or a bogus cop, more than an honest cop.

I had learned about bad cops when I was still a rookie. I was assigned to a guy who had a reputation as a "ghost"—he was always disappearing when there was work to be done. After roll call, he would drive immediately to a coffee shop. We wouldn't stay there ten minutes for a cup of coffee. That's acceptable, though frowned upon right after roll call. Instead, we'd be there half an hour while he flirted with the gals. Another one of his bad practices was to stop at the dairy and see if he could con the night man out of a quart of milk.

It's especially difficult for a rookie to be paired with that kind of partner. I'd be ready to do some police work, really chomping at the bit, and I'd wind up waiting in a cafe for him to get through flirting. Yet, he was supposed to be my training officer, teaching me to be a good cop. To me, it was an unending waste of time. We were goofing off, not looking for bad guys.

About three a.m. one morning, we were rolling down the street. *We're finally on patrol* I thought to myself as I looked between houses for prowlers or anything suspicious. He abruptly pulled up in front of a house and turned off the lights. I thought he had seen something. As he was getting out of the car I scanned the area and said, "Where is he?"

"You mean *she,*" he said with a grin. "Honk if we get a call."

I was still not sure what was going on until he rang the buzzer and some gal in a negligee greeted him. I knew then that I was really in trouble. If the sergeant came along, I'd either have to lie or admit that I was covering. Neither option was to my liking. This wasn't how I wanted to shape my career as an L.A. cop.

I sat there for a while, praying that something would happen. *How did I get into this mess? Lord, please give me wisdom.*

The radio broke in with a code-two urgent call for us. I really leaned on the horn and Bill came running, putting on his gunbelt as he came. I could tell he was really mad.

"What's the matter?" he yelled.

"We got a code-two."

He cussed and crawled into the car, and we went to a shop where the burglar alarm had been activated. We couldn't find anything. Later, as we were driving along, I decided to tell him how I felt. I knew it was going to be hard, because he was my senior.

"Bill, we need to talk. I don't want you to do again what you just did to me."

"What are you talking about?"

"Well, number one, that gal."

"Hey, Vernon. I'm not asking *you* to do *nothing.* If I want to make it with a few gals on the side, that's my own business. And if you don't like it, that's your problem, not mine."

"Wait a minute. It's your business if you're off duty. When it's on duty and I'm your partner, it's also my business. I would have been in trouble if the sergeant had rolled up. There's no way I'll do that again."

"What do you mean?"

"The next time you try it, I'll ask the sergeant for a new partner. If he wants to know why, I'll tell him."

"You wouldn't do that."

"Yes, I would. It's not that I'm going to fink on you, it's just that I'm telling you now, out front, that if you do it again, that's what's going to happen."

He was sore for a while. Pretty soon though, he said, "Okay, Vernon. You're right. It is unfair. It won't happen again." It didn't.

My training for that encounter began long before I entered the police academy. When I was seven years old I came home with a new reflector on my bicycle. My dad noticed the reflector and asked where I got it.

"From Donald."

"Did he just give it to you?"

"Yes, sir."

"Where do you think Donald got it?"

"He stole it."

"You took stolen property and brought it home?"

"Dad, I didn't steal it."

"But, son, you knew it was stolen."

"Well, I do now, but I didn't when he first gave it to me. Besides, I didn't tell Donald to steal it; I had nothing to do with that."

"Well, now that you know it's stolen, don't you think it's wrong for you to keep it?"

I thought for a minute. I really wanted that reflector and I hadn't stolen it. "No, sir."

He took me out behind the garage where there were apricot and peach trees. We had plenty of dry branches that could be used as switches, but this time he didn't select a switch. Instead, we sat down on empty apple boxes and talked for about forty-five minutes.

I was hard to persuade. When straight reasoning wouldn't work, my dad began making up stories. "Suppose your skates were stolen and given to someone else..." That changed the perspective and I soon got the point. He was determined not only to convince me that keeping stolen property was wrong, he also wanted me to understand *why* it was wrong.

Finally I said, "Dad, I've got to take that reflector back."

"I'll help you."

We hopped into the car and drove over to Homer Street and Donald's house. Dad waited while I went around to the back. Two other friends were there. I went up to Donald and said, "Here's the reflector back."

"What's the matter?"

"It's stolen."

"You knew that!"

"Yeah, but I got to thinking it over, and it's not right."

"Oh boy, did your dad talk to you?"

I nodded. They laughed, and I turned around and walked back to the car, my ears burning, and almost in tears. Instead of heading home, my dad drove down Soto Street. Every time I asked where we were going, he just shook his head. He slowed down and turned into the Sears department store.

"What are we doing here?"

Again, he would say nothing. He led me into the bicycle area.

"Pick out any reflector you want."

I couldn't believe it! I chose a great big fifty-cent one, the kind with marbles in it. When we were back in the car and headed home he said, "Son, I don't approve of your taking stolen property, but you were honest and you made things right. That's important."

I've never forgotten that. When I think of my dad, dead now for several years, it's one of the best memories I have. Dad was an L.A. cop, and back then they only got three or four days off each month. With so little free time, most dads would have spent their day off with other adults going to a ball game or fishing or doing something else they wanted to do. My dad shared his time with me. He took half of his day off to reason with me over a lousy fifteen-cent stolen reflector. I love him for that.

His concern for me to learn to daily develop the trait of honesty has stuck with me. That characteristic is so important in a cop, and I soon found that most of the men I was to be teamed up with were helpful, committed, regular guys. However, as in any large organization, there were a few odd ones, even in positions of authority. One of those would soon have an impact on my career.

5

A PATROL-BEES TO BANDITS

One day after Bill Shirley and I sent a suspect to jail, Bill said he had an afternoon court case and suggested it was a good time for me to drive up to the academy and qualify on the range. I agreed. If I failed to report before the end of the month, I would be subjected to the penalty of a day off without pay. I had just completed my six-month probationary period and I didn't want any disciplinary papers in my file.

Having completed probation also meant I was authorized to drive a radio car alone. I checked out a black-and-white from the pool, feeling a sense of machismo and pride at my new status. All the way to the academy I felt obvious and visible. It was fun watching drivers exhibit symptoms of "black-and-white-itis." I remember one car burning rubber to stop for a caution light. He stopped smack in the middle of the intersection, then pulled away sheepishly. As I eased onto the freeway and headed for the tunnels north of Chinatown, several speeding cars slowed to regulation speed. As soon as a motorist would see me in his rear-view mirror, his brake light would go on. It was an unconscious reaction.

When I drove through the academy gate, I read a sign indicating that officers with odd-numbered serials were shooting on the 25-yard range this month. Being an even, I would shoot on the combat range. The parking lot was crowded, indicating that many others had also waited until the end of the month.

As I walked up the stairs to the range-master's window to pick up my thirty rounds of ammo, I saw classmates Williams and Terry in line. Terry was a short fellow. He barely made the minimum of five-nine and he said he had done stretching exercises to reach that. But what he lacked in height, he made up for in coordination and tenaciousness. He was an all-around athlete, active in sports and bodybuilding disciplines. Our names were together near the end of the alphabet, so we had often lined up side-by-side during academy days for the physical training drills. Even though I was six-three and at 210, outweighed him by 35 pounds, I learned very soon to respect his combat wrestling skills.

Terry grinned and called, "There's the old flatfoot. How's it goin', big fella?"

"Great. How about you guys?"

We talked as we picked up our ammo and filled out our qualification cards. We walked together to the line and waited for the next relay.

"Have you heard that several from our class will be on the next transfer?" Williams asked.

"No," I said, "Seriously, are they thinking of moving some of us already?"

"That's the word," Terry explained. "They want to move us into the outlying divisions to make room in the action divisions for some more graduates."

"Boy, I hope they leave me alone," I said. "The last thing I want is to go to a slow area."

"Next relay, move in!" The loudspeaker broke up our conversation, and we moved through the safety gate.

The first test was at seven yards. Two strings of five rounds fired in three seconds at hydraulically-turned targets simulating the silhouette of a man. More than ninety percent of all police gunfights take place at close range. The next position was ten rounds at a target fourteen yards away. All shots were fired double-action without pulling the hammer back. In each instance we practiced point shooting without using the sights. Last was a barricaded position behind a small wall twenty yards from the target. In this situation, the sights are used and careful aim is taken.

I found it difficult to concentrate. I kept thinking about the possibility of being transferred away from a foot beat in Central Division. As I wiped my weapon clean of the powder residue with the rag provided behind the barricade, I checked the three targets to see how well I had done. At twenty yards, I could make out at least two clean misses on the seven-yard-line target. I had placed a five-point arm shot in the fourteen-yard-line target. The rest appeared to be in the kill zone. Later, when I picked up my qualification stub, I found I had yet another shot outside the kill area. Even so, I had qualified.

After a cup of coffee with Williams and Terry, I headed back to the Barn. I found Shirley getting his shoes shined. I held up my qualification stub. "Well, I did it, but just barely."

As he squinted at the scores, I said, "You know, I think you really need glasses."

"Looks like you're the one who needs the glasses. You usually shoot better than this, don't you?"

"Yeah, I guess I was preoccupied. I heard that some of us are being transferred."

"Hey, maybe that's what Sergeant Heinrich wants to see you about."

Shirley kidded a lot so I wasn't sure if he was serious or not.

"Does he really, Bill?"

Shirley nodded.

I couldn't get into the watch commander's office fast enough. Sergeant Heinrich looked up and said, "Vernon, I've got good news for you." He stood up and motioned at the green sheet metal assignment board on his cluttered desk. All forty-seven magnetic nametags of day watch personnel were scattered about among paperwork. With a grin, he said, "Well, no more parking problems or freeway driving. We're transferring you to Highland Park Division."

"Highland Park?"

Sleepy Hollow, an old man's division. I guess he could read my disappointment.

"You *do* live just a few blocks from Highland Park Station, don't you?"

"Yes, but. … well, I like all the action here."

"Look son, there's police work in every division in the city," he remonstrated, raising his bushy, grey eyebrows and wrinkling his forehead. "There's more to police work than arresting prostitutes and pimps or working the drunk wagon. You can work just as hard in Highland Park Division if you want to. The work's different, but it's there. Many of the bandits that caper down here live up there, and burglars are a dime a dozen. You'll have more time to do discretionary work, get involved in traffic enforcement and chalk up some juvenile experience."

What he was saying made sense, but I wasn't buying it.

"Look Vernon, it's best for you and us. You need a well-rounded training experience and we need to make room for probationers coming out of the academy. Don't forget the convenience factor."

He picked up a pink memo and handed it to me.

"You'll be on the transfer Wednesday. Call this sergeant and he'll tell you when to report."

I slunk down the corridor to the shoeshine stand where Bill Shirley was just stepping down and fishing for some change.

"Hey, Vernon. You got a quarter you can spot me?"

I handed him one without saying a word. He handed the quarter to the trusty, turned to me, looked me over, and asked, "Is something wrong?"

"Yeah."

"Did Sarge have bad news?"

"Yeah, I'm being transferred to Highland Park Sleepy Hollow."

"Aw, no kidding? Look Bob, I had no idea that's what the sergeant wanted to tell you. If I had, I wouldn't have pulled your chain like I did."

"Sure Bill, it's okay. I just don't... "

"I know, you enjoy walking beats. But maybe you do need a change of pace."

Bill continued mixing condolences with attempts to cheer me. But he saved a word of warning for his parting remark. "Watch out for the captain there. He's a little strange."

Several days later, I walked up the side staircase to the Highland Park Station. The beige, two-story brick building was in good repair for its age. Built around 1920, it had the classic police station look, with light globes on either side of the entrance. Inside, there was a hardwood-framed, glassed-in counter and high ceilings.

I checked in with the desk sergeant. Because roll call was an hour off, he had an officer assign me a locker and show me around the facility. After the tour, he took me into the watch commander's office to fill out cards for the emergency mobilization file. While I was standing there, a middle-aged man in a grey sharkskin suit walked in, greeted everyone with a perfunctory "Good morning," and without slowing went into an adjoining office. One of the morning watch sergeants got out of his chair, winked at the officer who was conducting my orientation, and walked to the door of the office the grey-suited man had entered. "Captain," he inquired, "would you like to meet one of the new men we got in the last transfer? He's from Central Division."

"Indeed I would. Send him in."

The sergeant motioned to me. "Come in, Officer Vernon, and meet the captain."

The captain's office was carpeted and had floor-to-ceiling drapes. He had removed his hat and was seated behind a large walnut desk. A conference table sat next to the desk. Not knowing where, or if I should sit, I stood awkwardly rotating my cap in my hands while the rather distinguished man scrutinized me. I suddenly remembered my personnel file and offered it to him. Without a word, he took it and began examining my papers.

"So you come from Central Division."

"Yes, sir!"

"Well, that's too bad," he scowled. "You've been broken in all wrong. Now we'll have to retrain you."

I assumed he was joking, trying to put me at ease. I shifted into a more relaxed stance and smiled. "Yes, sir, I'm ready to learn how to do it right."

I continued to study his pinched facial expression, waiting for him to break into a grin. Instead, he raised an eyebrow and pulled his head back, obviously perturbed at my making light of what he intended to be a serious comment. 'I'm not joking, officer. You see, in Central Division everything is handed to you on a silver platter."

I snapped back to attention. He noted that and continued his lecture.

"In Central, crime is open. You don't need to look too far to see it happening. The hustlers and knife fights, the shootings, B-girls, drunks, con men—they more or less run into you down there. You would have to be pretty dumb not to see them. We need men to handle those types of situations, too. But they should never have sent you, a recruit, there first.

"Up here, we have to dig and scratch for good arrests. There's plenty of crime, but it's not easy to spot. To be effective, it takes more commitment, more skill."

He got up, went to the window, pulled back the drapes, made a peephole between the slats of the venetian blinds and peered out, as if to survey his domain. He turned back to me. "I haven't seen a young officer trained at Central make it good here yet, and I don't think you'll be the first."

There was a knock on the door. A policewoman peeked in and apologetically explained, "Excuse me sir. I have that personnel complaint investigation report you wanted to discuss with Inspector Kingston. He's on extension three now. Would you like to speak to him?"

The captain, resentful of the interruption, tightened his jaws and snorted. "All right, I'll talk to him." Then, returning to me, he said, "That's all for you right now, but remember, your work will be closely scrutinized."

"Yes, sir!" I managed to say with conviction. I was so anxious to get out of the office, I almost ran-over the policewoman. After begging her pardon, I thanked her for rescuing me. "He was really on my case!"

She smiled. "I just couldn't take it, the way those clowns put you on the hot seat just for laughs." She gestured at the sergeant's office. "But it did take some thinking to come up with a quick excuse to get you out of there."

"You mean you set that up?"

"I called the inspector and told him I had the captain on the line," she said, a big grin filling her face.

Again, I told her I appreciated it. "By the way, should I take the captain seriously? He's a little strange, isn't he?"

She hesitated. Then, carefully choosing her words, she said in a low voice, "Well, some say he's a little psycho. He comes down hard on goof-offs, and usually rightly so. But on the positive side, he does recognize and appreciate good work."

As I headed for my first roll call in Highland Park, I was determined to prove the captain wrong. Whatever it took, I would cut it!

I don't know if his contempt for Central Division was authentic or not, or if he really was a little bit psycho, but his put-down worked on me. After that first meeting, I was determined to be one of the best cops he'd ever have under his command. I took the challenge seriously and never worked harder.

Roll call at Highland Park Division was similar to the roll calls at Central Division. The only difference I noticed was the lack of a formal, stand-up inspection before we were dismissed. Having judged the captain to be a stickler for form, I was surprised at the omission.

The roll call and unit assignments were followed by a crime briefing. Then came a reading of "wanted" teletypes and stolen car license numbers for us to write in on our printed L.A.P.D. hot sheet. Next, and finally, a discussion of changes in the vehicle code, coupled with an explanation of departmental policy on enforcing them.

The lieutenant, a black man in his late forties, stood by the door looking us over as we filed out. Later, I learned that every few days he popped surprise stand-up inspections just to keep us honest.

I was assigned Unit 11L75, a one-man radio car. The first digits indicated the division. Highland Park was the eleventh station established by the city. The letter "L" was the designation for a one-man patrol car, and the final digits indicated the geographical area I would be patrolling.

My orientation guide had given me a set of "car plan" maps. Today, there would be eight radio cars working within the division, so I examined the eight car plan to get a handle on the boundaries of my district. I still wasn't sure, so I decided to wait until I got outside.

I followed the crowd down the stairs and got in line at one end of a ten-foot-long counter. Two officers were working the public station desk, assisting a couple of citizens in reporting crimes and helping another who was obtaining a bike license. One desk man had arranged field crime report notebooks and shotguns on the counter for easy checkout. While waiting in line, I again examined the car plan maps. An older officer, standing in front of me, turned and stuck out his hand. "Vernon, I'm Stan Shultz. I work 11L49, the car just north of your district."

"Nice to meet you, Stan. I'm trying to figure out my district. Maybe you can help."

"Sure thing. Lay the map on the counter here and I'll point out your boundaries. Have you worked a radio car much?"

"No," I admitted. "I just transferred in from Central. I've walked beats and worked wagons most of the time."

"Well, look. I'll try to roll on some of your calls. And if I'm tied up and you need some advice, call one of these other guys. We're all here to help."

Two other officers joined the conversation and offered their assistance. The shorter one said, "On day watch 'L' car, you'll get quite a lot of crime report action. If you have trouble, use your field crime report book. It's laid out pretty well. Just take your time and do it by the numbers. You'll make out all right."

"Thanks. I'll call if I get hung up."

Turning out of the station driveway, I had mixed emotions. I liked the feeling of piloting my own ship, but there was a lot I didn't know. I switched on the radio and practiced giving my unit number several times. Then I depressed the transmit button. "11L75, clear."

The operator acknowledged, "11L75, clear."

It was nice knowing that in the communications dispatch center downtown, operators could now see a green tab displayed under my unit number. 11L75 was ready for calls.

The first call came immediately. Apparently dispatch had been waiting for the day watch to clear before transmitting a report on stolen property. Four hubcaps taken from an elderly lady's car. It was simple enough and within half an hour I cleared again and started driving around the district, making mental notes of key intersections as points of reference. Thirty or forty minutes passed, and then my number crackled, "11L75, 415B, 3711 Dunbar Avenue."

"11L75, Roger," I acknowledged.

I pulled up to the curb and stopped. I didn't know where Dunbar was, but I soon located it in my Thomas Street Guide. It was situated in the hilly southeast corner of my district. But what still puzzled me was the call itself, "415B." As I turned the black and-white around and headed toward Dunbar, I reaffirmed my recollection that a 415 was a disturbance, an argument, or a fight. A major 415 was usually a gang fight. But what was a 415-B?

I drove up a steep hill, spotted 3711, turned the wheels into the curb, and shut off the engine. Not knowing what to expect, I grabbed my nightstick and slid it into the ring on my utility belt. I started up the cement stairs toward the house, which was obscured by the grade. I could see people on the porch of the house to the south, and they appeared to be agitated.

There were fifty or more steps that switched back and forth as they climbed up and over the old cement retaining wall. Breathing hard, I arrived at a white frame house.

A white-haired, disheveled lady was on the porch, brandishing a broom. "Thank goodness you're here! They're out in back; that way." She pointed toward a walkway on the north side of the house.

"Who's out in back? What's going on?"

"The bees, the bees! And they're mad! They're stinging everybody." She waved the broom. "Do something."

"Okay, lady, I'll do something." *But what?* To buy a little time, I sought confirmation of her complaint. "You mean you've got bees out back? Honey bees?"

"Yes, bees are out there. The kind that sting."

"Wait here, I'll take a look," I said. Walking up the narrow, brick walkway, I figured out the signal the operator was saying, "415, bees." But now that I understood the call, what should I do?

At the corner, I could hear them buzzing. They were upset, all right. Cautiously, I peered into the backyard. About twenty feet beyond the back of the house was an apricot tree. Under one of the lower limbs were smoldering pieces of burning wood and cardboard. Directly above, sagging from the limb, was the largest swarm of bees I'd ever seen.

"There they are," she said. She hadn't waited out in front, as I had asked, but had walked back through the house to the open rear porch. "Shoo, shoo! Go away!" She swatted at mavericks with her broom. I brushed several bee bombers from my face with my hand as I ran to the back door and pushed the lady inside.

"Let's get in here and make plans, okay?" I said, closing the screen door behind us. In my memory banks, I found no entry under "bees." In that regard, our academy training had been deficient.

"How did this happen, ma'am?" I asked, stalling again.

"How did it happen?" she repeated incredulously "I don't know. I just looked out about an hour ago and there they were."

"Well, I mean, who built the fire and made them mad?"

Defensively, she admitted she was the one. "But I intended to drive them away. Instead, they stayed and got mad."

The doorbell rang. I followed her through the kitchen, dining room, and living room. She opened the front door, and there stood Stan Schultz. "Oh, good," my hostess glowed. "It's another police officer. Maybe he'll have a good idea. Come in. Come in."

"What's going on, partner?" Stan asked as we walked into the kitchen. "A swarm of bees," I explained. "They're really mad. She tried to drive them off with a fire. What do we do?"

Schultz leaned across the breakfast table to peer out the window. "Yep, they're mad all right," he grinned. "Do you know who they belong to, ma' am? Do any of your neighbors raise bees?"

"No. All of my neighbors hate bees. They've tried to help me get rid of them. They haven't the vaguest idea where those critters came from."

Removing his notebook from a shirt pocket, he flipped through its pages. "No problem," he said. 'There's this man who keeps bees, and when we run into bees and don't know who they belong to, he comes and gets them."

After a phone call and a short wait, the "bee man" arrived in his panel truck. He put on his special hat, which had a veil of netting hanging from the brim. He slipped into a jumpsuit, pulled on some gloves, and minutes later climbed into the back of the truck with the bees swarming all over him. He had found the queen and kidnapped her, and the colony had followed. Like a wise policeman, the guy had quieted a bunch of rowdies without a scrap. Stan's solution, which he had put into play so quickly and effortlessly, was based on experience and common sense.

Working Highland Park wasn't always as easy as calling the bee man. Those days of car patrol taught me the importance of being in the right place at the right time. One day, I was patrolling solo in a radio car near Avenue 44 and Figueroa. A man in front of the Union 76 gas station was waving at me and pointing down Avenue 43. I headed that way, and as I rounded the corner, another man pointed to the Pasadena Freeway. As I approached Carlotta Boulevard, an access road alongside the freeway, a third man who was standing on the corner pointed in the direction of the boulevard.

Once on Carlotta, I saw the reason for all the pointing. A man in a gas station uniform was chasing a fellow who was clutching a sheaf of bills in each hand; a clue that even a cop can figure out. I parked and joined in the chase, forgetting to report in.

The chase had already proceeded for about four blocks, so I caught up with the bandit pretty quickly. When he saw me, he threw the money from one hand at me and reached under his belt for something. I could see the glint of a metallic handle of some type, but I couldn't tell if it was a gun or a knife. I could have shot him, but I was so close, I felt confident I could be onto him and bring him down before he could turn on me. I reached in my pants pocket for my sap, a billy made out of a leather pouch filled with lead. I struck him on the side of the head with it. He fell and the money fluttered onto the street. As he fell, I saw that his weapon was a big screwdriver with a metal handle.

He was knocked out, and I handcuffed him. As he started coming around, I dragged him to my car and opened the back door. Just as I did, I heard my unit being called: "11L75, 11L75. Tilltap of service station at Avenue 44 and Figueroa. Just occurred. Suspect wearing black trousers and red sweater…"

I grinned at the holdup man and reached over in the front seat and got the microphone. The operator was still broadcasting, "…last seen running toward the Pasadena Freeway."

I broke into the transmission. "11L75. Suspect in custody."

"11L75. Repeat, please."

I repeated. Again, she asked for it.

"11L75. I have the suspect in custody—the guy with the red sweater." I doubt that she believed me, even then, but she didn't ask me to repeat again.

The man from the gas station was effusive with praise. "Boy, you got him good. I couldn't catch him, and I didn't know what I'd do if I did."

When we returned to the service station, the owner was excited. "It's fantastic! I can't believe it! I had just hung up the phone and there you were! This modern police department, with all its scientific advancements—it's amazing!"

I didn't have the heart to tell him what had really happened.

6

A PACT FOR SURVIVAL

Fernando J. "Nick" Najera had an uncanny sixth sense. He could spot a crime before it happened. Or, if we arrived while it was in progress, he instantly scoped out the situation. At interrogation he was a master, playing hunches and applying practical psychology. His street knowledge came from having grown up in the barrios of El Paso, where his high cheekbones and squint evoked the nickname, "Indio." As a teenager, he rode the rails to Los Angeles. After service in World War II Nick became a cop, and he already had ten years of experience when we became partners.

Fortunately for me, Nick was one of my first partners and the best teacher I could have hoped for. We worked a felony car, which was the only plainclothes patrol assignment on the day watch. It was good duty. We didn't catch the garbage calls like family disputes, illegally parked cars and loud parties. Mostly we scratched up our own work with hardly any radio calls at all.

On the East Side, that meant that our most frequent targets were juvenile rip-off artists and hypes.

Ordinarily it was good duty, but on this particular day the midafternoon sun was really beating down and our unmarked Plymouth was almost unbearably steamy. The city officials permitted us to ride with our coats off, but still considered air conditioning a luxury.

"Only twenty minutes to go," Nick said, running a forefinger under his collar. "A day like this makes night duty seem attractive."

"We've had a busy one," I commented. "Three hypes off the street, two field interviews, and an AWOL marine booked on a petty theft warrant. I doubt if the hypes will be off the streets long, though. What do you think?"

"Ninety days, maybe less. Then they'll be right back shooting dope and capering to support their habit. We aren't likely to run out of work, for sure."

"Did you see that?" I asked. A skinny kid was coming down the outside stairs of an old hotel. When he saw us he paused, then ducked around the back. He fit the hype profile. The giveaway was the long sleeved shirt. On that scorching day, everyone but hypes and cops were in short sleeves.

Nick nodded agreement as I opened the glove compartment and pulled out the microphone. "Eleven-Frank-One, code-six at Avenue 24 and North Broadway."

By the time the dispatcher on frequency 13 had acknowledged my transmission, Nick had already pulled into a parking spot. Grabbing his coat he barked, "Take the back door."

We needed no further communication. I ran around the corner into the alley while Nick hit the front door.

In the alley, a second staircase jutted out from the upper story of the hotel and came down between two small garages. I had barely made the cover of the first garage when I heard a screen door bang open and someone running.

I flattened against the wall just inside the garage door and took a deep breath. I considered drawing my gun but decided I needed both my hands to stop him. An element of surprise should give me the edge, even if he were armed, which I hoped he wasn't.

Suddenly he was there. I grabbed a handful of shirt and slammed him against the garage door. "Police officer!"

A scared, frail kid cried out, "What's happening, man?"

"That's what I wanna know. Are you holding?"

"No, man. I'm clean, honest."

I quickly patted his clothing to see if he was armed. He wasn't.

Nick, having checked the hotel downstairs and upstairs, raced down the steps, stopping abruptly after almost running into us.

I finished the personal search. Nick held his badge inches from the youth's face and demanded, "Where do you live?"

"Evergreen."

"What are you doing over here?"

"I came to see a friend."

We both examined his eyes as he looked at the badge. They were down, pupils pinpointed. He'd had a fix. Nick continued the interrogation.

"What's your friend's name?"

I don't know."

"I thought he was your friend."

"Well, yeah, but I don't know him all that well. Actually, he's…"

"We know. He's your street gorilla. He just got through turning you on, right?"

"No, man. I'm clean."

I joined in. "Come on, don't give us that. Your eyes are down. You just shot up. Let's see your marks."

He hesitated, then started rolling up his right sleeve. Nick grabbed his left arm. "Let's see this one first." Nick grinned and said, "Partner, I wonder why he'd want to show us his right arm instead of his left?"

On the inner side of the elbow was an obvious ugly pin-cushion of scar tissue. Nick pulled out his handcuffs. A look of anguish came over the addict's face. "Hold on, man. Don't do that. I'm on parole. If I get busted, it's back to the joint."

Nick continued cinching up the cuffs on one wrist. "You tell us about the gorilla upstairs and we might let you skate this time."

We knew he would eventually tell us. At his level of existence, his only concern was where his next shot of dope would come from.

"Look. Will you guys really cut me loose if I level?"

Nick looked at me, then back at the hype. "We'll cut you loose as soon as we know you're telling the truth."

"You mean you're going to keep me until after you raid?"

"You better believe it. Then, if you're leveling, you can go. If you're lying, they'll stick you so far back in the can you'll never see daylight again."

"Will you keep me outta sight?"

"No problem."

He glanced at us head to toe, then whispered, "He's in number eight and he's holding pretty big. I think he just made a big connection. You guys will be promoted for this."

"Awright, awright. Cut the con. What's his name?"

"Gato."

"Gato? The Cat, huh?"

"Yeah, that's his street name. It's all I know. He's alone and he's got too much to stash fast."

"Is there a toilet in the room?"

He rolled his eyes around trying to visualize the room.

"I don't think so. Just a small sink."

We led him back up the staircase, screening him from view. Inside the back door was the common bathroom, typical of hotels built at the turn of the century. Nick handcuffed our hype-turned-informant to a water pipe. As wasted as he was, there was little chance he could break away.

"You want to change your story?" I asked. "If you're not shooting straight, it's going to be Trouble City, friend."

"Man, I'm leveling."

Nick gave the handcuffs a last check, then peered down the hall. "Let me do the talking. If we hear him trying for the window, we'll kick the door down."

We eased along the hall, stopping at the first two doors to look for a number. Neither had one. Nick was ahead of me as we moved down the hall on the threadbare rug that no doubt contributed to the musty smell. He stopped at the next pair of doors and pointed to the one on the right. I took my place on the left side .

Nick knocked twice, then spoke in a quiet, low voice, "Gato? *Abra la puerta.*"

I heard the bed springs squeak inside, then heard him walking towards us. I examined the door for the best place to kick it if he wouldn't open up. It wouldn't take much to bust it, I concluded.

When the door opened, I saw a middle-aged Mexican, complete with a Pancho Villa style mustache. Then I glanced down. In his hand was a .32 caliber blue steel automatic.

Street pushers never use guns. That's what they said. We had busted a lot of them, and they never were armed. Never mind tradition, though. Gato had a pistol in his right hand, and our pistols were in their holsters.

"Cops, huh?" The derisive tone of his voice and the smirk on his face made the .32 seem even more menacing.

Nick and I had sensed all along that the day would come when somebody would get the drop on us, but not a pusher. Every cop has to face up to that reality. Almost every day you make arrests, conduct searches, prowl back alleys. It's so easy to relax your guard, to neglect those precautions that are designed to keep you alive.

I wasn't going to surrender. Even if resisting or running or trying a ruse might end in my getting shot, I wasn't going to surrender and put my life into the hands of a pusher. Nick, who had earned the Silver Star for gallantry in action during World War II had convinced me that your odds for survival are better when your enemy doesn't have complete control.

"Look at it this way," he said. "If we get shot during a gun battle on our beat, somebody's going to call for help. We'll get extra guns or, if we've been shot, we'll get medical attention. But if some ding-a-ling takes us prisoner and decides to shoot us, it's likely going to be in some off-beat place and at a time of day when nobody's around. Maybe the bandit you surrender to won't hurt you if you cooperate, but I don't like the idea of trusting bandits."

My right hand was moving for my pistol, my left hand, tugging to get the bottom of my coat out of the way. A button popped off and glided through the air as if in slow motion. My gun hand wouldn't move fast enough. All I could think was, *I hope he shoots Nick first, giving me a little more time to protect myself.*

I knew Nick was going for his gun, too. Now my pistol was out of its holster and I was lifting it to aim at Gato. I couldn't understand why he hadn't fired yet. I was beginning to apply pressure on the trigger of that Smith & Wesson .357 Combat Magnum. Then Gato dropped his gun and raised his hands.

In a flash, Nick slammed him against the wall and searched him for any other weapons. I kicked the .32 across the floor to keep it out of Gato's reach. Then, while Nick handled Gato, I checked the place out to be sure he had been alone.

With Gato cuffed and the room secure, I realized how frightened I had been. My pulse pounded in my neck and my hand trembled as I re-holstered my gun. I was glad to be alive.

Our informant was right. His gorilla was holding pretty big for a street pusher. On a makeshift wooden box table next to his bed was a pile of white powder, a box of clear gelatin capsules, a carton of milk sugar and a few balloons. One balloon contained at least eighty caps of heroin.

With Gato cuffed to the headboard of the brass bed, Nick and I stepped outside.

"Bob, go ahead and cut loose the hype, but first make a field investigation card on him," Nick whispered. "And you better drop a dime and call into headquarters. I'm sure the ten minutes is up on our code-six. They'll be sending a black-and-white to check on us, blowing our cover. I don't want that to happen because I'm sure we'll be having some visitors very soon."

I checked on our informant and told him to take it easy. Then I went to the pay phone. The hall was so dark, I had to strain to see the dial. The light socket over the phone was empty. A tenant had probably stolen the lightbulb.

When I reported our situation to the watch commander, he asked me to hold. After a few seconds he came back on. "Okay, but I need your car for the night watch, so don't wait around for more than a couple of hours."

"Right, lieutenant. I'm predicting we'll run out of handcuffs and car seats pretty quick. We'll see you in a couple of hours for sure."

I told him we were holed up in room 208 and he promised to send a sergeant if we hadn't reported back within two hours.

I hurried to the toilet to free the informant.

"Did-did you get him?" he asked nervously.

"Yeah. But one thing—why didn't you tell us he had a gun?"

"A gun? Hey, man! Shut that door, will ya?"

"Don't panic. My partner has Gato cuffed in the room. We're going to keep our word. He won't see you leave."

"Can I go now?"

"Easy, man. Let's see something with your name on it."

I removed the handcuffs and he fumbled through his pockets. He fished out a wallet and handed it to me.

"Just give me a driver's license or some kind of I.D."

He found a social security card and I.D. as an outpatient at Los Angeles County "Generous" Hospital. As I made out the card, I told him to take off his shoes.

"Are you going to take my outfit?"

"That's right. You're going to smash it up and toss it."

From one of his shoes he removed a dirty, rolled up handkerchief. He handed it to me. In it was an eyedropper, a needle, and a spoon with most of the handle cut off. Stuck to the spoon was a piece of brown, fibrous material.

"What's this in the spoon?"

"Oh, that's a piece of cotton."

"What's it for?"

"It's a strainer. You know, when I cook up some stuff, I pull it up into the eyedropper through the cotton."

No wonder addicts get abscesses and hepatitis. The whole outfit had a putrid smell. This poor guy actually thought the dirty cotton strained out germs, or perhaps it was just part of the ritual.

"Okay, now break it up."

I handed him the syringe and eyedropper. He stomped on them, and I tossed the spoon into a trash can. I finished the F.I. card. I couldn't release him without saying something about his addiction.

"Have you ever wanted to kick your habit?"

I'm not hooked that bad. I'm jittery a lot but I could stop if I wanted to."

Either he didn't want any help yet, or was too proud to admit it.

I told him he could go. He hesitated, glanced down the hallway, then he ran down the back stairs and through the alley.

I returned to room 208. After making sure the hallway was clear, I went in. "Everything under control?"

"Yep, did you...er..uh..." He looked at Gato. "Did you go to the bathroom?"

"Everything's okay now." I picked up Gato's pistol and removed the clip of bullets from its handle. "A cup of coffee says this piece is stolen, Nick."

"No bet!"

"How about a bet on whether it came from a house or a car? If it's from a car, I'll buy."

"You're on."

"Gato, where'd it come from?"

"Just before you guys came in, a hype gave it to me for a few caps. He said he won it in a crap game, but I dunno. Maybe he's a burglar."

Nick and I exchanged glances. No wonder our informant wanted to get away so fast. He wanted to be gone when we got around to asking about that gun.

"Do you mean you just got the gun before we came in?" I asked.

"Yeah. This strung-out hype didn't have any bread, so I took the pistol in trade for some stuff. He was hurtin' so bad, he shot up right here in my room before he split."

Nick was marking each capsule of heroin with his initials for later identification in court. I decided to ask Gato the question that had been bugging me: "Why didn't you shoot?"

Gato stared at me as if trying to get a read on why I asked. I had tried to be casual. Nick had taught me the benefits of being congenial with a suspect. Even with felons, friendliness and humor resulted in more openness, and ultimately more effectiveness on our part. I didn't press. Knowing Nick's approach, I figured he had established good rapport with Gato and may even have played down the seriousness of the incident.

"Hey, man," I shrugged, "it's no big thing."

Something else was still bothering me. Inside I was ashamed, and I had to get it out. "Nick, you know what? When we were going for our guns, I was hoping he would shoot you first."

I didn't know how Nick would react. Taking care of one's partner is a prerequisite for a cop.

A grin filled his face. "Yeah, well, you guess what was going through *my* mind?"

I felt a big load had been taken off my shoulders. I returned to the question Gato had evaded.

"Really, why didn't you shoot?"

"I don't know. Maybe because both of you went for your guns at the same time. One of you would have gotten me. Anyway, I was loading the gun when you knocked. I wasn't sure the clip was in right. It might not have worked."

"What if we had surrendered?"

He grinned. "I don't know. Maybe you don't want to know, either."

"Bob," Nick broke in, "we'd better get ready for visitors. With this much dope, he's bound to have some customers calling soon."

I moved over to the large window and watched the street while Nick instructed Gato: "When your friends come calling, you're not going to say anything except 'come in,' right?"

"Sure, man. I'm not going to hassle you guys. But you *will* tell my parole officer I cooperated, won't you?"

We didn't answer. Neither of us were interested in helping a man who made his living selling dope.

Fifteen minutes or so passed and I saw two young men crossing the street toward the hotel. "Hey, I think we've got two on the way."

Nick looked out the window. "Yeah, I think you're right. I don't recognize them, but they're hypes all right. Can you believe it, wearing long-sleeved Pendletons on a day like this!"

I was a little anxious. I doubted either of them would be armed, but I didn't have the foggiest whether they would submit to arrest, or run, or fight. I shucked my coat and threw it on the bed.

"Bob, stand by the door. When they knock, I'll open up and we'll both pull them in. If we don't create too much of a fracas in the hall, we can probably get a couple more without getting burned."

After what seemed like more than enough time, I began to

wonder if they were coming. Then I heard the hall floor squeak. Nick was quick. On the second knock, he jerked the door open and snatched one of the hypes into the room before I could react. The other one was back from the door, and he reacted as quickly as Nick had. I was out in the hallway and after him before he had much of a lead. I caught him at the end of the hallway. He didn't resist. I grabbed his right arm and turned him around. As I frisked him, I said, "Police officer. Are you holding?"

He shook his head. His eyes told his story—hopelessness. He knew he would go to jail, suffer withdrawal, do time, return to the street, then repeat the pointless little drama. Later, his record showed that he was 19 years old and had spent three years in institutions. He admitted to committing an average of three burglaries a day to support his habit.

I handcuffed him and started back to the room. I sensed that someone was watching. An obese woman in her early twenties, wearing a brightly flowered muumuu, was peeking out a cracked door. A naked toddler pushed the door open and eyed me curiously.

I pointed to the badge on my belt. "I'm a police officer. My partner and I are conducting an investigation. We'd appreciate you staying in your room until we tell you it's safe."

She nodded, pulled the child back into the room and closed the door.

Back in Gato's room I reported, "One woman heard us, but she looked too scared to do anything."

"Let's try again," Nick said as he shut the door.

After waiting another half hour we picked up one more hype and decided to call it quits.

Back at the station came the crucial part of the police work. Whether or not our arrests would stick depended on how carefully and how thoroughly we processed our prisoners, booked the evidence, and prepared the paperwork.

Three hours after leaving the hotel and eleven hours after

reporting for work, I slipped in behind the wheel of my Renault. As I started it up, I saw a couple of night watch officers going over the car Nick and I had driven, looking for any new dents. If there was any new damage, and we hadn't reported it, the liability would be on us. If there was damage and they missed it, it would be charged to them.

As I watched them, I reflected on the events in the hallway of the hotel. Even the memory of those few seconds started the adrenaline coursing through my veins again. I took a deep breath. I now had time to evaluate what had happened. Not only had I come face to face with the probability of my own death, I had committed myself to a course of action that would have meant my taking a life. I *had* put pressure on the trigger—ready to fire. Was that Christian?

Then I recalled the passage of Scripture in Romans 13 where rulers, or policemen, are referred to as ministers of God and that they do not "bear the sword for nothing." I told myself that this work is not only compatible with Christianity, it is biblical and therefore it is God's work. At least it should be.

While Nick and I were still working a felony car, two other officers, Collier and Stanislawsky, joined us to work dope. The addicts in the area were responsible for most of the crimes against property. I teamed up with Stan, a classmate at the academy.

We were watching a dope dealer's house to try and build a case on him when we saw two hypes come hurrying down the street. They were sniffing and obviously hurting and needing a shot. They entered the house, stayed twenty minutes, and came out cool.

After they had walked a couple of blocks, we pulled alongside and scooped them up. Their eyes were way down, pinpointed; in fact, they were so out of it that as we talked to them, one kept nodding out.

"Both you guys are on parole, right?"

It was slow coming, but they both gave an affirmative answer.

"Are you in a drug abuse program?"

"Yeah, but we don't have to take a urine test until next week."

"You guys give us the drawings on the house, showing where he's holding, and we'll let you skate. Otherwise, we call your P.O. right now."

"Hey, man. We can't do that."

We twisted them a little. "It's either you or him. He's making money off your misery. What makes you think you owe that kind of loyalty to him?"

After several go-arounds, one said, "Okay, man. Where's a piece of paper?"

He drew the inside of the house, detailing the bathroom. "Here's the toilet, and here's where he stashes it in the flush box. When you guys come in, it's going down the toilet."

"We'll take care of that. Listen, if you guys are blowing smoke at us, we'll pick you up and charge you in violation of parole. But we're going to let you skate now because we think you're leveling."

We let them out of the car and called the other unit. At that time, all you needed to enter and search a house was probable cause, which we had. Two hypes had just made a purchase and had told us the guy was holding.

Our plan was for Collier and Nick to cover the outside; Stan would go in the back door and I'd enter the front. The two guys on the outside would stand at diagonal corners and watch the windows. If somebody went out the window or threw the stash away, in court we would have to be able to identify specifically who it was and say that we saw it happen.

I went in the front room and, just like the hypes told us, there was a TV and a bunch of kids on the floor watching it. According to the hypes, they were the pusher's nephews and nieces. When I went in, they looked around but didn't seem too concerned. I asked, "Where's your uncle?"

"He's in the bathroom. He's not feeling too cool."

As I made my way down to the bathroom, I met Stan in the

hall. I pointed to the bathroom and he nodded. We braced our shoulders against the opposite wall and kicked the door open. The impact shorted the bathroom light loose, and it went out like a strobe light. In a split second, I glimpsed the suspect, sitting on the toilet. He had a belt pulled taunt around one arm to make a vein pop up. He had just punched the needle in and was shooting smack when we broke in. His heroin, bundled in a bandana handkerchief, fell onto the floor. The doorknob hit him right in the nose, bringing blood.

From the drawing the hypes had given us, we had anticipated a regular-sized bathroom, but it was more like one of those portable johns used on construction sites. In the dark, I dived for the dope on the floor and managed to get six bundles into my pocket. In the meantime, Stan was struggling to keep this guy from putting the dope in the toilet. They were grappling on top of me. When the toilet flushed, Stan yelled, "He flushed it! He flushed it!"

They were hitting each other and yelling. I got excited and started shouting, "He flushed it!" forgetting I had six bags in my pocket, which was all the evidence we would need.

I managed to get to my feet to try and help Stan. It was pitch dark, and we were flying off the walls hitting one another.

Nick and Collier heard us yelling and came running in, jumping into the ruckus. Now there were five men doing gymnastics in a room built for one to sit. Finally, I yelled, "Choke him out! Choke him out!" I heard an "Urrrrrgggg."

"All right, bring him out in the hall where we can see him."

Nick, who is really bullish and strong, backed out with his victim. It was Stan, and he was out cold. The pusher, meanwhile, was crawling out the back door on his hands and knees. His nose was still gushing like an artesian well. We regrouped and grabbed him quickly.

When Stan came around, he said he knew it was one of us who had done the choking, and he accused each of us in turn. We wouldn't say which of us did it.

Stanislawsky is retired now. A drunk driver ran into him and his partner. Their vehicle was hit with such force that the front seat broke apart and Stan and his partner were hurled into the back seat. Stan's back was permanently injured and he was given a medical retirement. Today, he's a taxman and he prepares mine. Every time I meet with him, the first thing he says is, "You were the one, weren't you, Vernon?"

7

THE DELICATE BALANCE

The radio gave the description of two bandits who had just held up a store.

It was another instance of being at the right place at the right time. As the description of the car was being read by the dispatch operator, it passed by us.

Nick spun a U-turn and we pulled them over. I jumped out, gun pulled, and headed for the driver. When I opened the car door, I told him to get out.

"Get outta my face, copper."

He didn't move and continued to sit with his hands on the wheel as if I hadn't said a word. Since they had just committed an armed robbery, I knew they had guns.

When he refused to move I grabbed his coat and yanked him out. As I did, he gave me a sharp jab while his buddy went for a gun under the seat.

"Hey, Nick! He's going for his gun!"

I let loose with a left that knocked the driver up against the car. As he started to swing back, I kicked him hard and he crumpled up as he fell to the ground.

Nick had his gun aimed at the other guy's head, and I came over from the driver's side and pointed mine. "Leave it there, buddy."

Slowly he drew his hand out from under the seat. My partner reached in and pulled him out of the car, putting the handcuffs on. The man I had hit was coming around. I handcuffed him. We put them both in the back seat and radioed in.

I didn't realize it, but one of my Sunday school students, Eddie, had seen the whole encounter. There were more than ten kids in my class and I knew they each looked up to me as their teacher. I was trying to be a good example. I would tell them a few cop stories and weave in something from the Bible. They really took it in and Eddie was one of the regulars.

But the Sunday after the arrest of the holdup men, Eddie wasn't there. Nor was he there the next two Sundays. When I did run into him I said, "Hey, Eddie, I've missed seeing you at church. Where have you been?"

He looked up at me square in the eye and said, "I don't want to come to your class anymore."

I stopped and bent down to him. "What's wrong, Eddie?"

"You're a dirty fighter!"

"What do you mean, Eddie? What are you talking about?"

Then he explained that he was on the corner to pick up his newspapers when my partner and I had stopped the bandits. "I saw you kick that guy. That's dirty fighting."

I explained about the guns. It was a fight for life. I needed to protect my partner in case the other guy started shooting. He never bought my explanation. To him, it didn't matter. I was a dirty fighter, a bad cop. In his mind, good cops never drew first and never fought dirty. They were always stronger, benevolent and kind! The bad guy might kick and bite and pull hair, but not the good guy. He fought by the rules, completely straight.

This popular image, encouraged by television, is that the bad guys take turns poking at the hero. If they are fighting with swords, the bad guys stand in reserve and when one of them gets through, another one jumps in. In real life, bad guys don't wait their turn. They do it all at once. They do a number on you. If you don't fight back in kind, you are not only going to lose a lot of fights, you will probably wind up in a hospital, or dead. In real life, the good guy would be beaten, killed, or maimed. He wouldn't make it home that night.

But because it was Eddie, I let it really bother me. I knew that what I had done in that situation was not brutal or unnecessary. It was a matter of survival. Yet Eddie had misunderstood. The crucial thing now was how I responded to myself about his charges. Would they continue to gnaw at me inside or could I appropriate them as one of the realities of being a cop?

Being a policeman is a daily struggle for balance—walking the thin line as both a cop and a peacemaker in blue. Hopefully, if you get off-center, there will be someone to point you back on track. Usually when it happened to me, a good friend let me know.

One night Don Botsford was riding with me when the radio was cleared for pursuit of a motorcycle thief. I joined in and soon was standing over the body of a 19-year old.

"Well, that's one thief that won't make parole," I said.

I took a long step over his crumpled body and headed for the car. A few minutes earlier he had ditched five cars in pursuit. Then, with his light off, he had whistled through a stop sign and hit a station wagon broadside. The force had turned the wagon around.

Later in the car, my friend asked, "You realize what you said back there?"

"Naw. What'd I say?"

He looked incredulous. "You mean you step over the body of a 19-year-old boy and make flippant remarks about parole and you don't even remember it?!"

I hesitated a moment and bit my lip. I was tempted to retort, *That boy you're talking about had stolen a motorcycle and was resisting arrest. At least ten men were involved in a high-speed pursuit. Any one of them could have been killed, not to mention the innocent citizens in that station wagon who are in the hospital!*

Instead of offering my rebuttal, I took a deep breath and let out a sigh. The longer we drove the more I thought about it. What my friend shared I eventually realized was true. I had tipped over. Later, I thanked him for his help and insight.

Through that comment and other experiences I began to learn the importance of working hard at keeping a proper perspective. It's easy to insulate oneself from normal feelings and emotions, to build up the proverbial callous and to become cynical.

My role as a cop gave me an off-balance exposure to life. A cop is called when something is wrong. It might be a thief, a dishonest employee, a runaway, a drunk, a child-beater, a prostitute, or someone just being obnoxious and in a fight. It is easy to begin thinking that all people are like that because that is what composes a cop's daily routine.

I began to recognize the need for positive encounters with individuals. It was important to establish friendships with people other than cops. In these associations, I was often unwittingly forced into a defensive position on law enforcement. I would have to listen as they talked about the bum ticket they had been given by some arrogant cop, or the classic, "How come you guys are never around when I really need you?"

My wife, Esther, and I became sponsors of the high school department at church. That helped. There were over a hundred kids, most of whom had their heads really screwed on right. Having social gatherings in our home and witnessing this crime-prone age group having a great time without getting stoned, but rather, experiencing acts of kindness, honesty, and love by truly committed Christians provided much needed balance to my perspective.

I continued to learn that a good attitude is a crucial element in the performance of a cop. One day I went to an apartment complex in search of a male suspect in his late sixties. He probably wouldn't cause any trouble. He was named on a crime report, accused of molesting a three-year-old and four-year-old in the next apartment. He hadn't been around since the alleged incident. The detectives working the case had asked me to check the apartment as often as I could.

This time I decided to stop and ask some of the neighbors if he had been around. There was movement and lights in the apartment directly across the walk from the suspect's apartment. I pushed the buzzer, knowing the occupants were already up, even though the hour was quite early. Both husband and wife came to the door, apparently seeing my uniform through the curtains and wondering why the police were calling. Yes, they had seen the old man last night and were quite sure he was inside.

I crossed over the lawn and pushed the buzzer—no response. I hit it again. This time a shade moved. "Police officer. Open the door, Mr. Shapiro."

"Just a minute. I'll be right there."

At least one full minute went by. I could hear movement, but no one opened the door. Just as I was about to knock again, the door began to open. It wasn't the man I was after. This man was too young; thirty-five at most.

"Good morning. Is Mr. Shapiro home?"

"You mean my father, Leo?"

"Yes, Mr. Shapiro."

"No. He's been away for over a week."

He was lying! It was all over his face.

"Are you sure he's not here?" I asked as I scanned the layout of the apartment. "I'm going to have to talk to him sooner or later."

As my eyes moved across the kitchen area, I saw the morning sun coming through an open door in the service porch. *An open door!* I stepped back off the porch and walked quickly between the apartments. A car was already pulling out of the driveway and onto the street. I trotted to my car, jumped in, fired up the engine, and quickly pulled away from the curb. I stopped him eight blocks away.

Mr. Shapiro, the alleged child molester, was on his way to jail. Knowing the details of what was contained in the crime report, I detested him. I'm sure I revealed my dislike in my facial expressions, tone of voice, and general demeanor. Reacting to my attitude, he didn't say much on our way to the station—just politely answered my few questions with a single "yes" or "no." He denied the allegations, saying the little girls were lying about him.

When we got to the station, I took the suspect upstairs to the detectives. Sergeant Flanigan was happy to see that I had apprehended him, but then came the big surprise. Flanigan treated him so nice! He smiled, called him "sir," bought him a cup of coffee, invited him to light up a cigarette, sat down and began casually talking with him.

I guess I was obviously displaying my shock and dismay over the way he was treating him because about halfway through the interview, Flanigan got up and asked me to step outside for a minute. As we moved into the hall he said, "Look, Vernon. I don't like child molesters any more than you do, but I've found that if I treat them nice, if I treat them civilly, if I treat them like people, it makes my job easier. Remember, our job is just to apprehend and conduct an investigation, not to punish, not to censor. All I'm trying to do is to find out what happened."

Before he could finish I butted in, "Yeah, but he just molested a couple of little girls. The things that he had them do, they'll never forget. It may affect them for the rest of their lives. That could have been my little girl, your little girl."

"Right, Vernon. And that's all the more reason I've got to get a good investigation going here, including a statement from him, hopefully. Then the courts can really deal with him."

We stepped back into the room. He continued his nice guy approach and within thirty minutes had a complete confession and a signed statement admitting to practically every detail that the girls had alleged.

My training officer, Nick Najera, tried to teach me the same lesson. He was congenial with all the bad guys in the neighborhood, waving at them as we were on patrol, stopping by and just making small talk with them. The strange thing about it was that they all liked him, even though he probably put more of them in jail than any other cop in the division.

One morning Nick and I were driving into the courthouse parking lot. We were discussing very important details of the case that we were about to testify on and unaware of what was going on around us. Suddenly loud yelling from across the rows of cars drew our attention. As we turned around we saw a guy in the distance happily waving at us. We instinctively waved back not realizing at first who he was. Then my memory kicked in.

"Wasn't that Goofy, the guy we're looking for on that robbery-rape caper?"

"Yeah, that was Goofy. Swing the car around and let's pick him up."

It was Goofy all right, and we did pick him up. He was hot and he wanted Nick to be the guy to arrest him. He knew Nick would treat him fair.

Even after the arrest of a suspect, the friendliness continued. As we would show up in court to testify against a defendant, Nick would always walk up to their security box, reach over and shake hands, then ask how the county jail food was and how they were being treated. After Nick would step away, you could always see the prisoners talking to one another. The guy who had his hand shaken was important. He felt like he had some kind of status.

At least someone in law enforcement was concerned about him.

Nick carried over this type of attitude into every contact and during those early years he tried to make me understand the value of it. For a while we were broken up into one-man cars. I was assigned to 11L93, the Lincoln Heights car, and Nick had 11L75, the car that bordered on my area. Part of Lincoln Heights was overrun with gangs, and there was one gang which was probably more infamous than any other; the Clover Street Gang. I knew they were responsible for several murders and many assaults. They were generally known as really bad guys. I had seen them often on my beat, walking the streets, sometimes in groups of two or three. Up to that time I had not had the occasion to arrest any of them.

One day while having a cup of coffee with Nick, he asked me why I was mad at the Clover Street Gang.

"What do you mean, mad?"

"Well, they say that every time you pass by them in your radio car, you look at them real bad and scowl at them. They think you don't like them."

In retrospect I have to say that although the scowl was unintended, it wasn't really that I was mad at them. I was kind of afraid of them. I knew who on the streets was in their gang. I knew what they had been responsible for and I guess that I wanted to show them that I wasn't afraid, so I gave them the macho bad-look back.

Nick tried to tell me that if I ever had to arrest any of them I would get a lot further with them if I was a little bit more on the friendly side. He explained that didn't mean I was approving of what they did, or being easy on them when they did have an opportunity to be arrested, but rather I was being open and fair with them. He then suggested that I begin helping him coach them at the Downey Street playground in the flag football league they played in. I hesitantly agreed, and for the next few weekends assisted Nick in teaching them how to play football.

One night the playground director got us a bunch of free tickets to a Los Angeles Rams football game. Nick and I took about 30 of the gang members with us. That was at least one night that they didn't hold up anyone or do anything bad. At the stadium during the entire event we were on them like a mother hen over her chicks. But, they still ended up enjoying the opportunity to see an NFL game in person.

I didn't fully realize the results of that rapport building arrangement until several months later during basketball season. I had taken a moonlighting off-duty job to police a basketball game between two rival schools, Lincoln High School and Wilson High School. As I look back on it, I don't know why I ever accepted the job. I was the only cop there with several thousand teenagers from opposing schools.

Just prior to the game, the vice-principal of Lincoln High told me they expected a gang fight at half-time or right after the game. There was no way I would be able to contain any kind of a gang fight by myself, and yet there I was. Then I realized he had said one of the gangs was the Clover Street Gang. Those were the guys I had coached in football and had taken to see the Rams. As I saw them come into the game, I took them over to one side, spoke in low tones and told them that I had heard from a very reputable source that there was going to be a big gang fight.

They said, "Oh, there is?" with surprised looks, trying to conceal the fact that they were involved. I didn't tell them that I had heard they would be participating in the fight. I asked for their help and instructed that I would blow on my police whistle when I expected them to come to my aid.

"Do you mean we can fight legally, coach?"

"As long as you're fighting on my side, you can."

"Okay, you blow the whistle and we'll be on the way."

Of course, I didn't have to blow the whistle because they didn't get involved in any gang fight. They were sworn to help me if I needed them. The lesson began to take—being friendly toward the bad guys could help.

I guess no lesson Nick taught me hit home as much as his example with York.

It happened when Nick and I were patrolling near Wilson High School. I spotted a carload of kids coming toward us. The driver was leaning forward, a dead giveaway that he didn't have keys and was using a quarter to bypass the ignition.

"What do you think, Nick? Look at the way he's leaning."

"I believe you're right, but let's wait until he comes alongside us. When he sees us, he'll want to straighten up, but if he's holding a quarter on the ignition, he won't be able to."

Just as they got even with us, the driver jumped into the back seat. The car went out of control, jumped a curb, and hit a tree. All four doors flew open and everybody split.

As Nick quipped later, "Even to a cop, that was a clue that something was wrong."

He and I chased them, each catching one. Two got away. Back in the car, we ran the license number over the radio. It was a stolen car.

Nick had caught the kid who was driving. Immediately, we knew he was a newcomer. His New York brogue was so pronounced that we nicknamed him "York."

As we were driving to the station, I said, "Hey, York, what did you jump into the back seat for, man?"

"I may be from New York, but I know what's happening on the West Coast."

"What's that?"

"Everybody knows that the guy who's driving gets more time than the guy who's joyriding. I just wanted to be joyriding when you guys busted us."

He wasn't exactly right. The Penal Code, 487.3, describes "Grand Theft Auto" as to *permanently* deprive the owner of his vehicle. That usually is interpreted to mean taking steps to keep it, such as repainting it, putting another tag on it, etc. But 10851 of the Vehicle Code describes *riding* without the owner's consent as joyriding. It's not as serious as grand theft. York had received some guardhouse lawyer's advice that was only partially true. Because of it, he jumped out of the driver's seat when he saw the cops.

While we were making out the booking slip, we asked the routine questions. "Father's name?"

No father.

"Mother's name?"

He didn't have a mother either. He said he was living with his grandmother.

"York, we know you've got a mother and a father. Where are they? What are their names?"

"Well, my father split when I was a kid, and my mother is dead."

Then he gave their names. Later, we learned that York was living in Los Angeles with a lady in her seventies who couldn't control him.

After we left the station, Nick continued to talk about York. "That kid needs a dad," he said. "I think he could be pulled out of this if he had a father."

A few weeks later, we went to York's hearing in juvenile court. He was found guilty, and he was going to be sent to some kind of camp. To the surprise of everybody, myself included, Nick stood up and said, "If the court pleases, your honor, can you assign that boy to me? I'll try to be his father and raise him as my son. My wife and I don't have children, and we can give him a good home."

The judge was incredulous. "Aren't you the arresting officer?"

"Yes, sir."

The judge had never had this experience before. After conversing with the attorneys, he gave a continuance, promising to investigate further.

Caseworkers were sent out to talk with Nick's wife, his

neighbors, fellow officers and superiors. After all the information was gathered and reviewed by the court, Nick passed with flying colors. The judge assigned custody of York to Nick and his wife.

It wasn't all peaches and cream. On several occasions Nick had to take York back to juvenile hall. The youngster just wasn't used to being disciplined and ended up rebelling. Nick meant business though and he would take him back to court. Eventually York stopped resisting and began to shape up. Several years later York got a job and was married. As far as I know, he hasn't gotten into another scrape with the law. He writes to Nick and occasionally comes back for a visit.

I've seen those values in numerous policemen. They've provided kids with clothes from home. They've told them, "I won't file a petition on you if you'll come in once a week and show me your homework."

Often, when I'd go to the office on Saturday, I would see kids lined up with their notebooks to show the sergeant their homework. It wasn't police work, but he was just trying to get these youngsters to be somebody. There's a commitment beyond the forty hours a week and the paycheck from the city. For some young officers hoping for an assignment with juveniles, there is a desire to invest in kids and I was no exception.

I guess that's why I really was interested in catching dope pushers. Their biggest customers were teenagers with problems who turned to dope to solve them. Even then I learned the importance of treating them as people.

Alvin was another good example. We had been trying to catch him for months. He was an active dope seller, dealing so much that even the seven and eight-year-old kids in the neighborhood knew about him. If you asked, they would tell you, "Yeah, he's a pusher."

But the department had always come out zero. He kept his stuff stashed in the bathroom, and would hit the toilet and flush it before we could grab it. We began to put in a lot of time planning how we could catch him holding—in possession of dope—and do it legally with a warrant. We decided we needed a juvenile to make some buys from him.

Using a juvenile to help make an arrest and conviction is a complex matter. You can't take just any juvenile and send him in to buy dope; that would be considered contributing to his delinquency. First, you need a kid arrested for possession. Then, you get his parents to agree to work with you in the investigation. If he's a ward of the court, you have to get permission from the court. You have to show that he's going to be safe— there's no risk, because you'll have plenty of cover, and so forth.

Once you're over those hurdles, you give him marked money and send him in to make a buy. When he comes out with the dope, you get a warrant, go back, crash in and get the guy. Most importantly, you find the marked money.

We followed this scenario and were ready to move in and arrest Alvin. We had a "paper"—a search warrant—but it wasn't endorsed as a "no-knock" paper. The problem was to keep him from flushing his stash down the toilet before we could seize the evidence. The only way we could force entry would be if he refused to open the door.

We were sitting outside his place trying to pick up any pattern in his activities, like coming out to get the milk or the newspaper. If we could grab him while he was outside, he would have no chance to get rid of the stuff.

While we were sitting there, some kids ran up to Alvin's apartment, pounded on the door and shouted, "Open up! It's the police!" Then they ran. He opened the door and yelled at them. By then, they were half a block away.

My partner and I grinned. Now we knew what to do. We could go to his door, knock, and say in a childlike voice, "Open the door. It's the police." If he came to the door, we could grab him. If he didn't open up, we could force entry.

We tiptoed up the stairs and I knocked on the bottom panel of the door. In a high voice, I called, "Open the door! It's the police!"

"Get out of here, you brats!" Alvin shouted.

Blam! Blam! Blam! We kicked the door three times. It wasn't only the door that went in. The frame and part of the wall caved in. Alvin was lying on a lounge watching TV, and suddenly plaster flew all over him. We came charging through with our guns drawn. "Police officers!"

As we broke in, we heard a scream. I ran into the bathroom while my partner guarded Alvin in the front room. I couldn't find anyone. I came back, still looking.

"All right, Alvin. Where's the woman?"

"What woman?"

"The one who screamed when we came through the door."

"Man! That was no woman. That was me! Let me tell you, when you come charging through the wall, the plaster flying and your guns in the air, shouting, 'Police!' I knew you were for real. And I screamed."

We booked Alvin without harassing him. I had begun to learn that I was the arresting officer and not the judge.

Two years later I was in uniform on the street and I ran into Alvin. He was fresh out of jail. He looked at me, and I looked at him, but neither of us was sure who the other was. In my uniform, I looked a little different than the day I arrested him.

"Hey, man! Aren't you Vernon?"

"Yeah."

"I'm Alvin."

"Oh, *Alvin*. Yeah, I remember you."

He asked me to wait a minute. He walked over and talked to two big dudes. They walked toward me. I figured really quickly that I was in trouble.

"Vernon, didn't you kick down my door, and didn't the wall fall in, sending plaster all over the place?"

"Yep, I did."

He turned to the two guys and said, "See, I told you! This is the dude I told you about. Man, can he kick in a door! Vernon, I want you to meet…"

He introduced me as if I were a long-lost friend.

Bob's dad LeRoy Vernon-11th Machine Gun Battalion in WWI (Front Row-Center)

VERNON, R.L.

LeRoy Vernon, L.A.P.D. 1922-1942

Bob entering the Police Academy-1954

Bob's "class" entering the Academy-1954

Sworn peace officer-1955

Certificate of graduation from the Academy-1955

L.A. Times story-
Evidence following a
dangerous arrest-1957

PUZZLER—Officer Robert Vernon looks over pistols
and knife found on Frank Vejar when police arrested
him on suspicion of robbery. Vejar would not explain
why he was carrying weapons and a pair of handcuffs.
Times photo

WARNED ABOUT TRAINS—Richard Ramos, 2, is
warned to stay off railroad tracks by Officers Fernando Najera, left, and Robert L. Vernon after they saw
boy frozen on tracks, saved him from onrushing train.
Times photo

Front page L.A. Times-Nick and Bob save a toddler from an
oncoming train-1956

With Nick, confiscating an illegal marijuana plant as plainclothes detectives-1956

Assigned to work at the Police Academy-1958

Top (L) Promotion to Captain-1970. Top (R) Promotion to Deputy Chief – Youngest in L.A.P.D. history at the time-1973. Bottom (L) Promotion to Assistant Chief-1979. Bottom (R) Chosen "Renaissance Man" by Esquire Magazine-1988.

Cinco de Mayo Festival, Hollenbeck Division-1972

Served as a volunteer chaplain for the department-1970's

Riding along with Officer Carter to check out the "action" on the streets

On TV news in one of the most active divisions in Los Angeles

Visiting Nick, his training officer, years later

Staff press conference with the Mayor of Los Angeles, Tom Bradley (Circa 1990)

Presenting Dragnet star Jack Webb a pin in appreciation for his support of the L.A.P.D.

Backstage with "stars" Mariette Hartley and Charlton Heston

Bottom (L) Comedian Leslie Nielsen and Bob share a laugh
Bottom (R) With Dodgers manager Tommy Lasorda

The honor of meeting President Reagan in Los Angeles-1984

The honor of meeting President Bush with the L.A.P.D. staff-1989

Top (R) Sharing a laugh with Pastor Chuck Swindoll at a graduation ceremony for Biola University where Bob served on the Board of Directors-1982

Top (L) Providing protection for Billy Graham in L.A. on the 25th Anniversary of the 1949 crusade-1974

In Washington D.C. with his wife Esther and James Dobson of Focus on the Family

Chief Daryl Gates presents the official chaplain's badge with Pastor John MacArthur as guest (Circa early 1980's)

The Vernons and MacArthurs taking a vacation from busy schedules (Circa early 1980's)

NBC TV, "Youth and the Police"-1970

Participating in "Cops and Pops" night at the Hollywood Bowl-1971

Conversation with teens at Forest Home Christian Camp-1968

Bottom (L) Hosting a Christian talk show (KKLA). Bottom (R) In Russia teaching with Pointman Leadership Institute after retirement from the L.A.P.D.

Top (L) Dating Esther in his new '53 Chevy

Top (R) "Caught" and married-September 1954

Bottom (L) 35th Wedding Anniversary-1989

Bottom (R) 61 years of marriage-2015

The Vernons with daughter, Pamela-1956

The Vernons welcome their son, Bob, now a complete family-1959

25th Anniversary surprise party with Bob Jr., Pam
and her husband, Steve-1979

(L to R) L.A.P.D. officers: Steve (Pam's husband), Matthew (grandson), Bob and
graduate Ethan (grandson) receiving his certificate from Chief Beck-2018 Recent
law enforcement graduates not pictured, grandsons Jake and Mark.

8

LOSER PARENTS

Bill Lynch and I had been working plainclothes juvenile out of Hollenback Station, and at dusk we went over to the Wabash Playground. It was a hangout for kids with a lot of traffic in drugs and liquor. Some of them would bring their stolen cars over to show off, which made it easy to make an arrest.

Bill parked our unmarked vehicle and immediately we saw some kids in a car they obviously didn't own. We pulled alongside them and said, "Police officers. Pull the car over."

They floored it, and the chase was on. I could feel the adrenaline pumping as the operator at communications acknowledged my call. "4-J-1 in pursuit."

I knew she was at that moment pushing a button which turned on a red light over her station and rang a bell. A "hot-shot" operator, trained for handling emergency situations, would take over.

Soon he transmitted: "All units on all frequencies, stand by. Unit 4-J-1 is in pursuit. 4-J-1, go ahead." He then keyed open his microphone so that all units in the area could hear my input and the feedback.

I began reciting street names into the mike as we entered or crossed them, meanwhile describing the fleeing car. At the moment, the driver was only wanted for speeding. I gave the hot-shot operator the license number and soon he came back on, "4-J-1, we have confirmed the car you are pursuing is stolen." That meant we were now after a grand theft auto.

I kept flashing our powerful hand spotlight across their window, trying to keep them distracted. But as we headed up into the hills near the city-county line, Bill said, "I hope they know about the curve ahead, but they're not slowing down! Lay back, I think they're going to crash." They rounded the curve, ran along in the outside lane for seconds, began tracking on the shoulder, and headed for a telephone pole. As they hit the pole the car went up it, overturned, and plunged off the cliff, which we remembered to be a two-hundred-foot drop.

They've had it. This is the end for them.

Bill braked hard and fifty yards beyond, the patrol car stopped. He and I looked at each other with expressions of shock and resignation. Before I got out, I picked up the mike and said, "4-J-1. The car we were chasing just went over a two-hundred-foot cliff. Requesting fire department, heavy equipment, and ambulance. Code-six, this location," and hung up.

Suddenly we heard, "All units. 4-J-1 just went over a two-hundred-foot cliff." And then he gave the address. Did he think I was broadcasting on the way down?

I broke in and clarified the situation. Then we went back to see what it looked like.

An incredible thing had happened. When the car hit the telephone pole, the left front fender tore loose the tension cable, tying the two together. Somehow the cable caught on the wheel or the axle and prevented the car from going all the way down the cliff.

It looked scary. The car was lying on its side. Then the driver's door opened, and one of the kids climbed out onto the car and looked around. I put my flashlight on him and he started sliding off the car.

"Come on up this way and we'll give you a hand," I called.

"No thanks! I'm making it!"

I flashed the light down the ravine. "Do you know where you're making it to?" I asked.

His eyes followed the beam. "Gimme a hand, will you?"

We helped him and his buddies up the embankment, cuffed them and took them to the station.

The next day I was out at the academy for my monthly qualifying, and I ran into Lieutenant Sunyich. He smiled and asked "How's L.A.P.D.'s youngest juvie?"

"Wishing I had it as soft as you academy instructors do."

"Vernon, if you were out here, what would you do?"

"I'd teach them how to be a juvie in two years!" I quipped.

"I bet you would, too, Vernon. I bet you would."

Just as we started to walk away, Captain Iannone came by. "Captain," Sunyich said, "we have an applicant for that teaching spot."

I turned ghost-white. Joking with the lieutenant was okay, but kidding the captain was out of my league. He asked me a few questions, then walked away. The following Wednesday, the transfer list was posted. Officer Bob Vernon, who began as a flatfoot and then became a radio car officer, a felony car officer, and a juvenile officer, now was Instructor Vernon, Los Angeles Police Academy.

I got cold feet when I saw it. Also, I felt a twinge of regret. I thoroughly enjoyed what I was doing, I loved chasing bandits, catching burglars, busting dope dealers, and all the other dimensions of working the streets. To go to a classroom for a teaching assignment seemed far removed from all that. Yet, I knew it was a good move. I was flattered and fortunate to be chosen.

The ensuing eighteen months at the academy were momentous in my life and career.

Without that experience, I'm confident I would never have been able to qualify for the advancements that soon came my way. The academy was like a prep school for the Sergeants' Merit Exam held every two years. It's a toughie, with both oral and written tests. After the test, a list of the scores are published. When a vacancy arises, the person with the highest score is promoted to fill the spot. At the end of two years, the list is wiped clean. New tests are given and the process is repeated.

Of all the tests I've taken—sergeant, lieutenant, captain, commander, and deputy chief, none was more difficult than the exam for sergeant. It's the first hurdle and includes the principles upon which the later tests will build. For that reason, it's not unusual—indeed, it's more or less expected—for a candidate to take the test a second or third time.

What my academy job did for me, apart from what I learned while teaching, was to motivate me to prepare for the sergeants' test. The academic atmosphere encouraged a study discipline that I never would've developed had I stayed on the streets.

Eighteen months after I took the academy teaching assignment, I was on the list to become "Sergeant Bob Vernon, L.A.P.D."

When I did make sergeant, one of my first details was detective on the night watch. My task was to do only preliminary investigations. In homicide, that meant you were the first to see and smell the body.

One of the worst cases came after only a few weeks in my new position. When the call came in, Detective McClendon, who was in charge of the night watch, said, "Okay, Vernon. It's yours."

A green detective is sure to get the baddies, the stinkers. I knew it must be bad or he wouldn't have given it to me. I got in the car and drove up to Montclair. The neighbors had noticed a terrible odor coming from the garage for the past several days.

In that same period, they hadn't seen the man who lived there, so they suspected he was dead in the garage.

The radio car was on the scene waiting for me. "Okay," I said, "let's raise the garage door."

"We already tried, but something's holding it shut. It's not locked, but it won't open."

"Come on. Let's give it a good yank."

We all muscled it together and suddenly the door shot up. A body fell onto the floor. It fell apart, intensifying the putrid smell. Maggots started crawling everywhere.

The man had hanged himself on a rafter next to the door. He'd stepped up on a little stool, then kicked it away. His body had blocked the door.

When a body has been in a room for two weeks in 80-degree temperatures, the stench knocks you for a loop. Detectives tell me there's only one thing that will clear your nostrils—a good jolt of booze. I've never tried that, but I do know that without it you can leave the scene and still experience that stench. You get out in the wind, and it's still there. You go to eat, but you can't. The smell's still there.

The coroner's unit pulled up. These guys really see bad stuff; a lot more than policemen. Two deputy coroners walked over.

"It's a bad one," I said. I was breathing through a piece of gauze that I had soaked in a sweet, citrus smelling solution that some ambulance attendants had given me.

"What's that?" one of the coroner's men asked. "You feel bad or something?" He grinned.

I shook my head and told them to hurry it up. I had to be right next to them, watching them get everything out of the pockets so that I could testify in court later, if it were relevant. This item was in his left pocket, that one was in his right pocket, and so on.

While I was observing their work, one of them said, "Okay, Bill, I got a cup of coffee that this one makes it to the wall first."

"You're on."

The maggots were crawling out of the body of a dead man and two guys were betting one another a cup of coffee on a maggot race. I've never forgotten that.

I've found that peer pressure is very strong in the police profession, especially the pressure to conform to the super male image of the macho tough cop. Often the impression given is that one must be tough to cope, hardened in order to survive. Mistakenly some cops feel that this toughness is expressed through coarse language, the ability to hold alcohol, or success in making sexual conquests. Being in areas where crime occurs and building effective communication with criminals on their level are some of the rationalizations used to justify, or even mandate "non-Christian" conduct.

This peer pressure has been difficult for me to handle. No doubt it's natural to want to be "one of the boys." At times I've felt very alone and on the outside when my Christian commitment has dictated a different lifestyle or kept me from participating with the group. Yet when I have yielded to His will, my relationship with Jesus Christ has not only given me the resolve and strength to stand firm, but has also given me the ability to cope and survive in a world of unusual pressures and experiences.

As a sergeant in the field, I felt that one of my functions was to motivate my men to do good, aggressive police work. When one of my men came to see me with a plan to catch some dope pushers and pimps during the dead time after 2:00 a.m. I jumped on it. His idea was to raid an all-night pastrami cafe that filled in the early morning with hustlers, pimps and pushers.

About 3:00 a.m. I called all units that were available. We decided to place one unit behind a fence in the alley that bordered the back of the pastrami stand. From their position the officers could see the rear of the cafe. It was important to watch the trash cans, which we had numbered. The rest of us met about five blocks away and split up into two teams, each ready to approach from a different direction.

On signal, we swooped down with flashing lights, sirens—the works. We made sure they heard and saw us at least a block away.

All who were holding contraband, like a gun or dope, ran around to the back and threw the items into the trash cans. Of course, they didn't know that there were officers in the alley looking through the fence, and noting who was throwing what into which can.

When we pulled up, I rounded everybody up and stood them against the wall. Then I backed up to the fence and listened to our guys.

They whispered, "The fellow in the purple shirt threw a gun in trash can number four. The guy in the yellow threw some over behind trash can number one. He missed, but it's back there somewhere."

I walked over to the cans and produced the stuff. "Okay, Officer Smith. Book *this* guy for this gun, and *that* one for dope," etc.

The suspects never figured out how we knew. What made it funnier is that we did it more than once. For some reason the word never got out that you don't throw stuff in the trash cans.

A lot of a cop's time is spent bringing people in on dope arrests. A tragically high number of these arrests are among kids. When working juvenile narcotics, I usually started the day out by visiting the office where I went through crime and intelligence reports about narcotic happenings around the city. Sometimes I interviewed juveniles who had been put in the detention facility by radio car officers for having dope. I was in the middle of a counseling session with a couple of parents and their son who had been caught at his high school campus with a large quantity of Seconal capsules—"reds" he called them—when my phone rang.

Excusing myself, I picked up the phone. I heard a young female voice on the other end saying, "Is this Sergeant Vernon?"

I said, "Hello. This is Vernon. Can I help you?"

Then I heard sobbing and crying. When she finally got her

composure I heard her say, "Sergeant Vernon, this is Kay. You remember me? You arrested me two weeks ago."

I said, "Yeah, I remember you, Kay. What's wrong? Is something happening?"

"Yes. Well, you told me to call you if I had any problems, and well, I do. Can you come over right now?"

"Well, tell me what's going on, Kay. What's happening?"

"I can't tell you. Just come over, quick!"

"Look, Kay. It will be a few minutes. I have to ... "

She broke in, "You gotta come over right now. My mom. She's out in the hall. She's been on a two-week binge with booze again and she's got half of her clothes on and she's having a fight with her boyfriend that she's been shacked up with for the last week or so! They're fighting over a bottle of wine and they've broken the bottle and they're cutting one another with it! Come quick!" Then she hung up.

Since I was in the middle of an interview, I called our communications division and dispatched a unit to the scene with the instructions that they were to call me after they got there. I finished my interview in about ten minutes and was leaving to go to Kay when the receptionist in the office called me over the intercom, "Vernon, pick up 01."

I picked up the extension. It was the officer I had dispatched to the scene at Kay's home. I asked him what was going on. He described a horrendous scene similar to what Kay had told me about over the phone. A drunken couple had cut one another with a broken wine bottle and they were half naked in the hall of the apartment building. There was blood all over the place. I told him to stand by. I would be right there.

When I arrived, I could hardly believe what my eyes were telling me. The poor girl's mother was badly cut up and the ambulance attendant was just loading her onto the gurney. The boyfriend was in another ambulance and on his way to the hospital. Inside the home there was blood all over the floor and walls.

Kay was sitting in the apartment with her head in her hands sobbing uncontrollably. After she got her composure she said, "You remember asking me why I used dope? Well, now do you know why?"

When you encounter rebellious kids, there is usually some problem in their home. Now, it's not always as dramatic and gross as Kay's home was, but there is usually something wrong.

My encounter with Ken is another illustration of trouble in the home. The assistant principal at Franklin High called and reported that Ken and his buddy had been selling marijuana. Mike Markus and I picked them up. Both were under eighteen, so we had to notify the parents. Since Ken's residence was between where we picked them up and the station, we decided to go by his home instead of calling on the phone.

On the way, Ken kept complaining that the laws were wrong. Marijuana was a good and healthy drug. It solved problems and it really helped him. For the first time, he said, he had found peace and happiness in his life.

"You're really happy, huh, Ken?"

"I really am. I've really found it."

When I pushed him he got angry and said, "Course ... I'm happy! Let's just stop talking about it."

When we reached Ken's house, I went with him while my partner stayed in the car with the other kid. Ken knocked on the door. No one answered. He had a key, so he opened the door.

"Mom's not here, but I think I know where I can reach her," he said.

He called a few places and finally contacted her at a bar. He told her what had happened, and I got on the phone and confirmed his story. She didn't seem concerned. I hung up. I was so stunned by the mother's disinterest, I suffered a lapse of routine precaution. I walked ahead of my prisoner to the door. Ken was a big kid, nearly six feet. When I reached out to open the door, he grabbed me by the arm and spun me around. I figured he was going to lay a Sunday punch on me, and I crouched to defend myself.

Then I realized he wasn't trying to hit me at all. He was backing away. He was tense, his face was flushed, the vessels in his neck were bulging, and his eyes were filling with tears.

"You want to know how happy I am, copper?"

I was so shocked, I didn't know what to say except, "Well, how happy *are* you, Ken?"

He stuck his wrists in my face. There were fresh, pink scars where his wrists had recently been sewn up.

"That's how happy I am," he wailed. "I'm so happy, I tried to kill myself." He dropped to the floor, sobbing. He was being arrested for peddling narcotics and his mother couldn't care less!

I've always felt the taxpayers of Los Angeles pay me to be a cop, not a preacher, but I reached over and put my hand on Ken's shoulder. I encouraged him to release the pain that was gnawing at his insides.

"There's a happiness that doesn't depend on drugs," I said, and I shared out of my own Christian experience.

When we reached the station, I called the chaplain at juvenile hall who was a good friend of mine. He promised to spend some time with the young man. Ken also shared that he'd like help.

Seeing kids like Kay and Ken helped me realize the importance of being a good parent to my children. The common denominator that I saw in all of these home situations was a lack of meaningful parenting during the formative years, which encouraged delinquency.

I've often heard from delinquents whom we arrested, "If my parents would only listen to me, if they would only talk to me, if they only loved me enough just to be with me for a while instead of always doing their own thing."

I made up my mind that I would carefully budget plenty of time to be with my children and my wife. I wanted to listen to them and talk to them. We needed to exchange ideas if we were to be a close-knit family.

One night when I came home and got out of my car, my son came running out to meet me as he often did. As we walked into the house I asked him what had happened with him that day. He came up with the typical "Oh, nothing." After I checked with my wife and found out that dinner wasn't going to be ready for about 30 minutes, I asked Bob to play a game of horse with the basketball. I knew he enjoyed playing. I went into my room and put on my grubbies.

We played for about 20 or 30 minutes. About half way through the game, just when I was trying to match one of his shots, he said, "I got in a fight today, Dad." My shot almost missed the entire backboard. Earlier he had said nothing happened, and now he was telling me about a fight. He went on to describe how he had torn this other boy's jacket in the fight on the bus and he was a little concerned about that.

I learned a principle from my son Bob that afternoon—it's important to spend time with your kids and to prove to them that you are ready to listen. We didn't start communicating until we were into that game, maybe 10 or 15 minutes. That's when the communication really started.

That kind of responsibility can easily lose its rightful place. When one's occupation involves many worthy causes, there can be a great confusion of priorities. A lot of cops become "married" to their jobs and end up losers in their roles as husband and father.

A guy can put in a lot of hours, chasing down a rapist-murderer, and feel completely justified in his commitment. But court time, call-outs for u.o.'s (unusual occurrences) such as labor strikes and disasters, added to regular duty time makes his time at home—other than to catch some sleep—sparse and unreliable. His wife and children begin to wonder which is more important, them or his job.

During my stint in Juvenile Narco, I listened to messed-up

kids talk about or refer indirectly to "loser" parents. It was then that I decided that my family would be priority number one. That took some discipline, some setting limits, saying no to some opportunities, and calling in a relief car when we were pretty sure the suspect we were waiting for was about to show. But I've never regretted that decision. I treasure our moments together as a family, and today my wife is my dearest friend, my married daughter is still "daddy's little girl," and my son is my best buddy.

9

SHOOT?

When I was about to make lieutenant they asked me to move to traffic. I really resisted. I sometimes thought it shouldn't even be part of the police department. They should turn it over to insurance adjusters or someone else.

Some cops enjoyed it, some didn't. I was one who didn't. My orientation was crime fighter, the cop after the bandit, preferably an armed bandit. Most of us didn't like burglars because they were sneak thieves, and mostly hypes. We didn't like forgers because that was too much of a cream-puff operation. But we had a healthy respect for an armed bandit. We figured he at least had the guts to go in and face somebody and risk a lot of danger himself. That orientation conflicted with being a lieutenant in traffic.

My superiors' response was that if I ever wanted to rise in the ranks of police work, I needed to take a serious look at that phase. They could have sent me without my consent, but they didn't want to force me. I finally agreed.

I had been lieutenant in the accident investigation division for about two weeks when the Watts riots occurred. Our division was immediately called on, as they are in any disaster, because they can suspend investigation of traffic and writing of tickets to form a ready reserve.

Ironically, the Watts riots took place on a Friday the 13th. I remember when Captain Tom Janes came walking into my office and said, "Vernon, there's some kind of a flap down on 103rd Street. Take half your watch and three or four sergeants and meet the field commander at the 103rd Street Fire Station."

When I asked what he meant by a "flap," he said, "It's between the citizens and the police. It may be bad."

We jumped into five cars with about six guys in a car and convoyed down. I have never forgotten the impact of turning the corner of 103rd and starting into Watts. The first thing I saw was a burning police car, upside down. Buildings were burning, bottles and Molotov cocktails were landing in the street. It looked like a war zone.

Once in the fire station, I discovered that another lieutenant, Charles Leonard and I were the highest ranking officers present. He had been a lieutenant for a month and two weeks longer than I. Until the department was fully mobilized, we were in charge. From our viewpoint, it seemed the city was coming down around us.

While Charlie was busy organizing the command post, an old-time sergeant came up to me and said, "Lieutenant, we've got to set up a perimeter."

"I'm not the field commander; Lieutenant Leonard is."

"He's too busy. If you don't do it, nobody will."

I hesitated for a minute. "Okay, Sergeant. Get me a map."

He brought one over and I said, "I'm sure we need a perimeter, but I don't know where. Where do I want a perimeter, Sergeant?"

"I've been out there and here's where I think it should be, sir." With his finger he drew the line.

"All right. Then that's where it'll be." I began detailing which men would be where while he took notes and marked the posts on the map. He implemented it, and two days later the perimeter was still intact.

All that day, the situation escalated. Our orders were twofold: try to contain the riot (don't be concerned to make arrests) and evacuate endangered residents. By three or four that afternoon, the riot was at its peak. The mob knew we were in the fire station; our police communications van was also inside.

When things were at their worst, one of the officers assigned to guard the facility told us the crowd out front was getting bigger and meaner, and they looked like they were going to do something. No sooner had he said that than a couple of Molotov cocktails hit in front of the door of the station.

It was clear that our security was severely jeopardized and something needed to be done. At most, there were a dozen of us inside. I knew that wouldn't be enough unless the psychological impact of a squad of trained regimented men coming out would scare them away. It was worth a try.

I explained my plan to the men and asked them to put on their helmets." Okay, we're going out by twos. The first four guys are to carry their shotguns at port arms. The rest of you get in double ranks. We're going in double-time on the count of three."

One of the overhead doors at the fire station had a smaller door cut in it. We would file out through it. The men lined up, ready to go. I could hear the mob outside. "We're going to go in cadence and in step, but you're to double-time on the count of three. Ready! One, two, three!"

The door swung open and out they went.

It worked. The show of power threw the mob totally off guard. They didn't know how many there were of us except that we kept coming out in twos. When the next-to-the-last guys marched out, 200 or more demonstrators broke and ran. Fortunately for us, they left behind their milk crate of Molotov cocktails.

It was a bad day for Los Angeles and Watts. The signs of the riot are still visible. Millions of dollars of damage was done, lives were lost, and injuries high. I recall seeing policemen with glass in their eyes, bricks smashed through windows, cars overturned, buildings destroyed, and the incredible looting was everywhere. It was a relief to go back to traffic duty for a while.

Not all of my stint as a lieutenant was taken up with accident reports. I learned about the heavy responsibility of sending men on details. Sometimes the best of plans could not prevent deaths.

A bandit duo had been plaguing one of the divisions. They were hitting dinner clubs and bars at midnight, robbing everybody and fleeing clean. I didn't have enough men to put a stakeout in each bar, so we developed a rolling stake, with three units covering six bars. We installed a rat's alarm in each bar. That's a tape transmitter housed in a little box the size of a pack of cigarettes. There's a button on the box, and when it's pressed, a prerecorded message is transmitted. The result—officers in a radio car hear: "Beep, beep, beep, number 26-beep, beep, beep, number 26." The number is the code for a particular location.

One night, the two bandits hit one of the places we had staked out, and the owner activated the rat's alarm. The duo had taken all the money and jewelry and put it in a pillowcase. Then, only minutes after the owner triggered the alarm, the gunmen herded everyone into a restroom. While that was taking place, the police rolled up in front and back, leaned over their vehicles' hoods with their shotguns, and waited for the bandits to emerge.

When the first bandit came out the front, the officers shouted, "Police! Freeze!" He had a pistol in one hand and his sack of "goodies" in the other. He raised his gun to take a shot and they cut him down with their shotguns.

The second bandit was in the doorway when the gunfire exploded. He ran back through the bar to the back door. When he opened it, the officers shouted, "Police!" He slapped his shotgun to his shoulder, but before he could pull the trigger they fired first, cutting him to ribbons.

Tragically, two people in the bathroom were too curious. A makeshift tool shed had been built onto the bathroom using three quarter-inch plywood. One wall of the shed butted against the outside wall of the john, covering one of its windows. Two patrons attempted to look out the window. Shotgun slugs pierced the plywood and hit one between the eyes and the other in the forehead. They fell back onto the floor flopping around with blood spurting from their heads in their final moments. The other occupants reacted wildly, creating pandemonium. Under the pressure of bodies, the door hinges popped off and the crowd piled into the barroom. It took half an hour to get everyone calm enough to obtain reliable information and piece together the true picture of what had happened.

One of the victims, it turned out, was the brother of a records clerk in the same division as the policeman who shot him. A sergeant called me at home minutes after the shootout and reported, "We hit one of your stakeouts, and we have some bad news. Four people were killed, and we think two of them were innocent victims."

Although television shows police officers always involved in shootings and using their guns right away, the extreme use of force is used only in rare occasions. In fact, one year the L.A.P.D. SWAT team only fired their weapons on five of over 200 call-outs involving a man with a gun. Most of the time they used alternative means; either talking it out with the person or using some kind of diversionary tactic. As a general rule, policemen don't like to use their guns.

The department even gives special recognition to officers who are involved in situations where they can legally shoot but choose an alternative that works.

One summer afternoon I responded to a request from one of my units for a supervisor; a code-three. It was at 46th and Broadway. A middle-aged woman had gone berserk. She had cut two people at a lunch counter with a twelve-inch butcher knife and was going for anybody who got close.

Officer Thompson had been hailed by citizens as he patrolled a couple of blocks away. When he arrived in his police car, she went after him. He had tried pulling his gun, but she wasn't impressed. He realized she was a psycho and called for some backup and for me.

Several other units were already there when I arrived. Some of them were keeping her busy as Thompson briefed me. He was tired, perspiring, his hat was pulled off and tie loosened.

"Boss, we got a bad one here. She's already cut a couple. Psycho and strong."

"Have you tried talking?"

"Yeah, but she's not buyin' that. Comes at us with that big blade and she's not bluffin'. She'll stick us if she can."

"How long has she been carrying on? Maybe she'll tire." As I spoke laughter shot up from the crowd of over 50 citizens. She had just charged the officers and sent them scurrying from the glistening knife as she beat the air with it.

"Making us look pretty silly, huh?" Thompson smirked, wiping his brow. "That's about all we've been doin'. Keeping her attention on us rather than them," he said, pointing to the crowd who seemed pleased to see one woman making fools out of four uniformed policemen.

"Come on, you guys. Do your job," one man taunted.

"I wonder what they want us to do ... shoot her?" Thompson responded. "Legally, we could, but we don't want to do that. What should we do, Boss?"

"Let's just keep doin' what we're doin', Tommy," I answered. "She'll tire after a while, and with our sticks maybe we can knock that knife from her hands. In the meantime, let 'em laugh."

For several minutes the scenario went on, almost like a bullfight, except not as graceful. She would charge and we would run, parrying the thrusts of her knife with our batons. Then it happened. She wasn't quite quick enough and several officers moved in with their batons, knocking the arm with the knife down and then against her body. Tommy jumped in and got a firm hold on the knife. As the rest of us moved in and grabbed her, he wrestled the knife away.

While the woman was being restrained, a cheer went up from the crowd and then applause. I shot a quick look at Thompson as he helped carry her to the car.

He grinned, "I guess they did appreciate our patience!"

I wrote him up for a Class-A commendation. That's real bravery.

Most of the times I've had to shoot, I really did it only as a last resort. At least twice I was extremely glad that I missed. That's probably due to what happened one day when I was working Lincoln Heights with Jack Collier. We had decided to patrol the industrial section, looking for weekend burglars. Inside a factory, we spotted a notorious burglar whose nickname was "Calles." That's Spanish for "streets." He was a heroin addict and, like most hypes, burglarized to support his habit. We were aware that there was a felony warrant for his arrest.

When he saw us, he ran. I hopped out and chased him while Jack followed in the radio car. Calles was known to be an exceptional runner. I learned he was also proficient at hurdles. He'd go over a fence and I'd go after him. By the time I was over it I couldn't see him. I would return to the car and we would continue looking for him. When I would see him again, I'd jump out, and before long he would have lost me again.

After losing him about four times, I was gaining on him when he took off alongside the Los Angeles River. Then he crawled over a fence. *If I don't get him now, I'm going to lose him for good.*

I climbed the fence and started around to the river. He had a good lead and it seemed I was going to lose him again. That's when I decided this was one of those cases where it was lawful for me to shoot. *He's wanted—there's a felony warrant out for his arrest. I've tried to run him down and capture him. Now we may lose him because we're down by the river and he'll probably go into one of the tunnels.*

As I continued to run, I drew my pistol and shouted, "Calles! I'm going to shoot!"

I had given him sufficient warning already. Several times I had called, "Police! Halt!" Still, for good measure I told him I was going to shoot. He glanced over his shoulder and kept running. I was looking down the sights—which isn't easy when you're running. I started to put pressure on the trigger. Pow! I ran into some bedsprings and fell. I hit hard on my elbows and knees. Through a big hole in my uniform I saw the skin was gone from one of my elbows. The knees of my trousers were also torn and gravel was ground into the skin.

I dismissed Calles from my mind, put my gun back in the holster, and started picking gravel from my knee. A shadow fell across me. I looked up, thinking it was Jack. It was Calles! He said, "Hey, man. Did you hurt yourself?"

Talk about feeling two inches tall. *Holy cow! I was going to kill this guy and here he's worried about my injuries.*

I put the cuffs on him just as Collier walked up. He really razzed me. "You couldn't catch him, so you pulled that act and won his sympathy!"

10

"OFF THE PIG!"

When I first made captain, I stayed in accident investigation for a short time. Then, in a little less than a year, I was sent out to Venice Division. Venice has been referred to by some city planners and sociologists as a microcosm of the city of L.A. This area includes ghetto, industrial, L.A. International Airport, a mixture of the hippie subculture and retired Jewish neighborhoods right at the beachfront.

Through the years, the varying lifestyles have greatly threatened one another, causing a lot of problems. The police were always caught in the middle. The hippies would get going on their bongo drums at ten p.m. just when the retired people were going to bed. They would call the police, and the police would have to enforce the curfew. The curfew stipulated that there were to be no loud noises after ten o'clock. Kids under eighteen had to have parental guidance to stay out after ten. Naturally, the hippies did not like that either.

This was only one of several factors which intensified the hostility in the community against the police. There were certain parts of Venice where rocks and bottles would be thrown every time a police car would pull in. The police would react, and soon there would be helicopters, more officers responding and a group of people going off to jail.

The situation culminated in an altercation in the Venice jail. One man lost an eye and other people were severely beaten inside the jail, allegedly by police officers. As a result, several officers were disciplined, a couple of other policemen were fired, and the captain was transferred. Because of the widespread publicity given the incident, a group of activists applied for a federal grant to act as a buffer between the police and the people of the community.

Captain Al Lembke was sent to the precinct. He was about ready to make commander, so he would be there only a few months. His mission was to take whatever steps necessary to get things whipped into shape. He set up administrative systems to ensure that the police were doing the right thing and that discipline was appropriate. He quickly transferred the police who were causing the most concern. And he did it before his promotion.

Now it was my time to command the Venice post. When we were talking about my assignment, Chief Davis instructed that he wanted me to bring peace to Venice and to lower crime. The framework was there, but the long-term implementation still needed to be done. The police and the community were poles apart and ill feelings were just below the surface.

These were big goals and the first year was pretty tough. There were a lot of confrontations, but I had an abundance of good help and advice from the people Al Lembke had brought in. Things were starting to patch up between the community and the police and crime was being slowed down.

One of the groups benefiting from the dissension didn't like the lowering crime rates. Simply put, their power base had eroded. Through our informants, we learned that certain individuals had decided I was the cause of it all and they were going to get me. The intelligence division was able to frustrate an attempt to bomb my office.

Another time, an informant came to the station and refused to talk to anyone but me. "Look. I'm an ex-con and I don't like cops. I just got out of San Quentin. But I don't go for a lot of innocent people being killed. There are some plans to get you, but I'm afraid they're going to get the whole station, civilian employees, cops, some prisoners in jail, and you. I don't buy that." We worked with him and again frustrated an attempt to bomb the station.

Later, we found they were trying to follow me home, intending to get me on the road, or at my house. Helicopters were dispatched to guard me.

Also during this time the County Human Relations Commission was holding meetings in various parts of the city to see how things were going. They announced they would have meetings in the Venice area on a certain date.

I knew the nature of the hearings and I wasn't afraid of them. They were going to sample the community and see how the police were doing. On the night before the hearings our intelligence officer, who had infiltrated the group that was causing trouble, told me some specific charges the opposition was going to make. The allegations were all lies, but they were difficult to refute with hard facts.

I honestly didn't know how to handle it. We had defused the bombings and dealt with the other threats, but how do you combat lies from people who don't know what's going on?

A lot of policemen won't share their trying experiences with their wives. It's natural to want to shield them from the gore, the filth, the way people misuse one another and the emotional impact that a cop sustains. That's not good. When people marry and become partners for life, they should share each other's experiences.

A policeman's marriage will have difficulty surviving if he always shields his wife from the sad and seedy. She won't understand the demands of the job. She will probably begin to resent his work because it is cheating her of her husband's time, interest, and commitment.

The night before the commission meeting, as Esther and I prepared for our regular devotions, I told her about the smear campaign. We had been reading the Bible, a chapter at a time, and that night's chapter was Psalm 75. Words and phrases jumped out at me…

"We give thanks to you O' God, Your name is near…men declare Your miracles…the earth and the people quake…You have set up the pillars of it."

To those of us who live in California, the possibility of earthquakes is very real. Yet, few of us give that threat much thought. On this night, when I read about the earth's shaking and God's miracles, I didn't think too much about it.

Although I was greatly concerned about the meeting the next day, I had decided there was little I could do about it. I said a prayer asking God's help, then went to sleep. I slept peacefully until 6:00 a.m. when the house began to shake. In fact, it shook so violently that my son Bob was thrown out of bed onto the floor. I tried to roll out of bed, and I was rolled right back in. After three attempts, I made it.

The quake continued for about a minute, which is a long time when the ground is shaking. Pam, my seventeen-year-old, came bounding down the stairs and jumped into my arms like a little girl. She was scared silly. When the shaking stopped, we gathered in the kitchen and turned on the radio. After a few minutes of no sound, a voice came on. "Ladies and gentlemen, excuse me. I ran outside. We have no doubt suffered an earthquake. We're waiting to hear what happened and will keep you informed."

The phone started ringing. The station wanted to know what to do. I told them to call in all the lieutenants and sergeants and I would be there as quickly as possible. Without stopping to shave, I jumped into the car and headed for the office.

When I arrived we immediately began to call in off-duty officers to send over to the valley. They were needed to help evacuate 80,000 people from their homes below a giant dam that had started breaking. We also had to set up anti-looting teams to take care of the vacated homes. A veteran's hospital caved in and a number of patients were killed. There were other deaths on bridges and freeways that collapsed. Homes were literally shaken off their foundations. The damage totaled several million dollars.

All my worry about the commission hearing had been unnecessary. A caring God had known that I would be caught up ministering to people whose lives were at stake at the very time when I thought my career would be under attack.

At the hearing that day, not one of the dissidents showed, so there was nobody to voice those charges against me. But the people in the community who cared stood up one at a time to talk about the changes and improvements. Later, members of the committee told me informally to keep up the good work.

I was reminded that my God was in control of the timing of the universe. The earth cannot shake or any of His children tremble without His knowledge.

My next task was to get the media to recognize what was happening. One of the principles that I had been taught in command school was the importance of cooperation with the media. Such communication was especially vital in a community having some autonomy, as Venice does.

The area newspapers were writing stories that, from our perspective, were anti-police. These stories included a lot of sensationalism about the confrontations between the police and the community. From reading the newspapers, one would conclude that the relationship between the two groups was worsening. It was, in fact, improving.

I began meeting with the newspaper publishers. My concern

was to get to know them and let them know me. I set up a monthly meeting with the reporters on the police beat. Over lunch, I explained the plans I had and the reasons behind them. If they were concerned about any police action of the past month, I tried to provide the police perspective. The intent was to bring them into an inner circle of knowledge and insight.

At first, the newspaper reporters were suspicious, though polite. I really convinced them of the sincerity of my intentions when I called them in on a raid. The vice squad had just completed several weeks of investigation on a sophisticated bookmaking scheme in the South Bay area. The setup was very commercial and included a big network of organized crime. As is usually the case, a lot of crime resulted from the bookmaking, especially in the collection of debts.

We were about ready to raid the top people in the organization, including the person who had the printing press at his house. I called the three papers and explained to them that I couldn't tell them what we were going to do, but I could guarantee them that it was newsworthy. I suggested that they each send over a photographer and a reporter to accompany us. Two of them did.

Those two were in on the raid from the start—the forced entry, kicking down the door, getting the evidence (the cards, the printing press), the whole bit. The raid received headline news. Apart from the impact of the story to the public, the reporters felt they were part of an "in" group. We had demonstrated enough confidence in them to let them go with us.

That raid really broke the ice for the police in Venice. People started feeling that *if I can trust them, maybe they could trust me.* What resulted was not a pro-police press, but at least there was a degree of objectivity that had been lacking. From then on, it was not unusual for the media people to call me, either to verify a story or ask for the police department's point of view.

When the media started having some confidence in the

police, they began communicating that attitude to the public. The stories were more objective. Gradually, the whole attitude of Venice began to be more open. To capitalize on the new spirit, we organized a community council that met every other month over lunch or breakfast. The group was composed of representatives of the various community groups, heads of certain service clubs, and several individuals who were openly antagonistic. The council's importance was vividly illustrated when we initiated a plan to reduce burglaries around the schools.

Through our reporting system, we noticed a high concentration of burglaries around the junior and senior high schools on the seven-to-four day watch. The pin maps we maintained showed this clearly. A red pin meant a day watch burglary, a red pin with a slash on it meant a night watch theft, and a red pin with a white dot a morning watch. Most of the pins were solid red pins and they were clustered around the school. It seemed obvious that most were probably committed by kids who should have been in school.

I decided to take the problem to the community council, show them the maps, and present a plan for resolving the problem. At the meeting I presented an update on crime and general plans for the future. Finally, I brought in the pin maps depicting the concentration of daytime burglaries around the schools. I explained the conclusions we had drawn. Their response was, "That sounds reasonable, but what is your plan?"

"Well, our plan is to conduct a school truancy sweep."

Their only negative reaction came when I explained that I wanted to bring in a couple squads from Metro—a tactical division of over 200 policemen who respond to specific problems in various areas of the city. I proposed that these squads pick up every school-age child not in school and bring them to Venice police station.

Arrangements had been made with the schools for their welfare and attendance officers to come to the station to interview each child. If the child had done nothing criminal and held no gun or dope, the welfare and attendance officers would call the parents and request that they take their child back to school. If there was cause to believe the child had committed a crime, we would fill out arrest forms and then call the parents.

This plan was presented in detail to the community council. They responded positively when they understood we were not going to give a record to every kid picked up cutting school.

The program was effective and pickups began to be made. There were some complaints. Some of the parents began calling the representatives of our community council, including some of the anti-police groups. "The police are at it again. They are picking up kids for no violation of the law. They're scooping them just for being on the street."

"Oh, we know about that," the representatives responded. "It's because of burglaries around the schools. Don't worry, the police aren't giving them records unless they are doing something illegal. They are merely turning them back to the schools. We support that."

Some of the disgruntled parents were pacified by that explanation. Even when they weren't, they didn't get any sympathy from the leaders. The system went smoothly and burglaries took a nosedive to less than half the number before the truancy sweep.

A division close to us tried the same plan, but without informing the community or bringing in public leaders. Their action resulted in an American Civil Liberties Union suit and a restraining order from the court prohibiting the police in that area from conducting any more school sweeps. This contrast reinforced my appreciation for the value of informing the public.

My final strategy in Venice was to work with the radical groups. One of those groups espoused violent overthrow of the government. They expressed this intent openly and had posters on their walls to prove it. One poster had an upraised fist with a gun in it. Printed over it was a quotation from Mao-Tse-Tung:

"To throw off the oppression of government, it is necessary to take up the gun and to destroy the oppressors." Below in bold print was "OFF THE PIG." That meant, "Kill the police."

This group had complained about police brutality and harassment. They charged that every time the police stopped one of their members or anyone visiting their place—no matter how minor the offense—the officers pulled a gun. Even for a traffic ticket, out came the gun. Their accusation was true, and to that group, "Baby, that's harassment and overreaction."

I went out to meet with the group at their place. I made a point of taking along a couple of bodyguards. I sat down and listened as they told me about the alleged harassment. "Man, even if the cops don't pull a gun, every time they stop any of us they put their hand on their gun or take the snap off the holster. It's the cops, the violence-prone cops, hassling us all the time, causing the problems."

After listening courteously I responded, "Well, I'll be honest with you. Because of the posters you have out here, I would do the same. I'm just like them. I see you to be a threat to my life."

"Come off it, Captain. We're no threat to your life."

"You can say that, but I don't believe it. That's why those two officers there came with me. I'm afraid you may try to kill me, and so are my men."

They looked surprised. "Do you mean the cops are afraid of us?"

"That's right. You say 'Off the pig' right there on that poster. You have a fist with a gun in it. Anyone would have to be pretty dumb to ignore that. Either you mean it or you don't. Until we have reason to think otherwise, we will believe you mean it."

"See, Captain. There you go overreacting. We don't really mean that we're going to go around murdering policemen for no reason. We will shoot in self-defense."

"Well, if you don't mean it, why don't you take down the posters? If you will, I think I can guarantee the policemen will stop pulling their guns unless you give them cause."

We tossed it around for a while and finally they agreed to try it. After they took down the posters I met with my men and told them, "They're taking down the posters. That means don't pull your guns unless you have to. Obviously, if you see someone reaching for a gun or coming at you with a knife, that's different. But don't pull your guns or even put your hand on your gun without justifiable cause."

To be honest, the men were not exactly pleased over the arrangement. Some of them said, "I feel uncomfortable without my hand on my gun in that place. Those people want to kill me."

I said, "They told me they don't want to, and maybe I'm naive, but let's try to meet them halfway. Part of being a cop is taking a risk once in a while. I'm sorry you're having to do it, but it's what I'm asking you to do."

The new arrangement began despite suspicion on both sides. There were no incidents. Before long this militant, anti-police group literally had some of their members walking the beats with police officers. They still were not in agreement with everything the police did and I'm sure part of the reason they agreed to walk the beats was to watchdog the police. But that didn't concern us because we didn't have anything to hide.

On a number of occasions, the presence of the militants diffused a situation. If someone wanted to resist a policeman who had an outstanding warrant for his arrest, the militants would help the officer. "Hey, man. This is a righteous warrant. The cop isn't harassing you. You gotta take care of this. Go with the cop and we'll get a guy from our organization to post bail."

Situations like that really impressed all of us. We found it incredible that militants who were "offing the pigs" only a few months before were now helping in arrests. I was convinced for the first time that even with militants of radically different political persuasions, peace could be made.

11

PUT ON THE VEST

Before I joined the L.A.P.D. I was not physically aggressive. My last fight prior to becoming a cop was probably in junior high. I knew that to be a good cop I would at times have to use physical force. Since I didn't drink or smoke or use profanity, I was concerned that people would think I was a softie and assume that I would fade in the crunch.

How would I react in a fight? Could I handle it? Could I be forceful enough? Those were the questions which plagued my mind as a rookie. I soon learned that police training and encounters with life-or-death situations brought my aggressive force quotient to its optimum level. The question which grew to be more prominent in my mind was, *what is the proper use of force?*

Sometimes my overzealousness has been detrimental, both to my Christian witness and to being a good policeman. I can still remember a bad rating I received. The captain said, "You are very goal-oriented and that can be an asset. But you are the type that says, 'Full speed ahead.' That can be admired if controlled, but you haven't controlled it. You've stepped on people and have been insensitive to their feelings."

I can still remember how that really hurt. My gut response was, *He doesn't know my true intentions. He doesn't know my sincerity. I don't want to hurt anybody. He's wrong.*

My initial reaction was to be bitter and dislike him, to transfer the guilt to him because I thought he had misread my good motives. I had gotten so "into" the aggressive demands of being a cop that the aggression carried over into my relationships with people.

While wrestling over it I remembered some biblical principles I had heard somewhere about accepting responsibility. The Apostle Paul was a very effective man because he accepted responsibility. He never rationalized or kissed it off to someone else. That stuck with me. Eventually I adjusted my attitude toward the rating report and what I initially thought were the result of my captain's misinterpretations of my good motives. I concluded that even if I were right, even if I had good motives, it is my fault that those motives are misinterpreted. He's only receiving the projection that is coming from me. I'm projecting the wrong image and that is my fault.

I began working on maintaining the right balance, and I'm still working on it. There have been times when I've blown it. But I've been encouraged by my study of the Scriptures that God will not allow me to be tested above the strength He will give me. (1 Corinthians 10:13) I do need help, and I've received lots of it.

Once you've seen the victims of rape or child molestation, once you have to inform a family their spouse or parent was killed by a drunk driver, once you have to explain to a mom-and-pop store owner that their savings are gone, you have no hesitation in wanting to catch the criminal. It's a righteous bust and you're glad to have a part in it. It's what I call "the victim orientation".

We received a call, a code-two emergency to the station from one of the call boxes situated on telephone poles throughout the city. The rationale behind having us phone in, rather than respond over the radio, rested upon two reasons: either the office was afraid someone was listening in on our frequency or the instructions were too long and involved for radio transmission. A long message was the case in this instance.

"There's a suspect in Curry's Ice Cream Store at Eastern and Huntington. The manager is positive the guy has a gun in his belt. He's been hanging around for at least two hours and has them all spooked. They're convinced he's going to hold the place up. He has a sack on the counter and they believe there's a gun in it."

The dispatcher described the suspect, told where he was sitting at the counter, and asked us to check it out.

When I returned to our unmarked car and filled Nick in, he said, "Well, you're up. You want to take it?"

I've always been gung ho. "Yeah," I said. "I'll go in and sit beside him. You sit near the door. I'll size him up, and then we'll go from there."

I walked in and took a seat next to the suspect. I hadn't anticipated the response of the employees. I lived only two blocks from the store and had often stopped there for ice cream on my way home from work. Even though I was in plainclothes, they recognized me. I sensed they were relieved that the cops had arrived, but they were uptight over what might happen.

"I'd like a chocolate ice cream soda," I said to the waitress as nonchalantly as I could manage. She turned to her boss at the cash register and asked, "Do we sell ice cream sodas?" I couldn't believe it was happening. There were pictures of sodas and signs advertising them all over the place. She was so flustered she couldn't think straight.

"Yeah. We have ice cream sodas," he said. "Fix the guy one."

She glanced at the fellow next to me while putting the ice cream into the glass and the scoop landed on the counter. I began to get uptight. I was afraid she would blow the whole scene. The suspect turned and looked at me, long and hard. I was relieved when he shrugged as if to say, "Now, ain't that a dumb gal for you?" When he turned and looked furtively in the other direction I saw the bulge in his coat. *I knew that tinker had a gun! I don't know what his caper is going to be, but I'm getting involved in a tight situation here.*

I drank the soda, fast. If I stood up without finishing, he would suspect something. I called to the waitress for my check.

"You aren't *going*, are you?"

"Yeah, my break's up and I gotta get back to work."

She handed me the check, stepped back, and put her hands behind her, a dead giveaway that she expected action. I guess the suspect thought she was upset that her boyfriend had to leave her. He didn't stir.

I took one step back; then I reached for the gun in his belt. If it *wasn't* a gun, I was going to have egg on my face. My fingers told me it was a gun. I let it go and grabbed both his arms at the elbows and pinned them to the counter. Rattled, I shouted, "Police officers! Keep your hands on the counter!"

I reached down and tried to yank the gun out of his belt. He came back with his elbow in an attempt to force my hand off it. I had a grip he couldn't budge.

I yelled at Nick, who was sitting near the door. "He's got a gun!"

People at the counter dived for cover. Nick took dead aim with his hog leg. I was wrestling to get the suspect's gun and get him off the stool. Finally, I worked him to his feet and jammed my pistol in his belly. "Another move and you're a dead man."

He hesitated, then raised his hands. I grabbed his gun and threw it over the counter. Nick came up behind him and began handcuffing him. Patting him down, I found handcuffs.

"Hey, what is this?"

"I'm a cop."

Instinctively I relaxed, but Nick shouted, "Keep your gun on him. I don't care if he's a cop or not, I'm not through cuffing him up yet."

The cuffs in place, Nick said, "Let's talk about this outside."

I picked up the sack lying on the counter. Another gun! Outside, when we demanded his badge and identification, he couldn't produce them.

At that point, the only charge we could arrest him on was illegally carrying a gun. But while he was in our custody, a sheriff's deputy recognized him from a wanted poster. He had robbed and kidnapped a young couple. After handcuffing them he drove them into the woods above Crest Highway. There he tied her boyfriend to a tree using rawhide and made him helplessly watch as he raped and beat the girl. When his sexual assault was done, the abductor rolled his victim over a cliff to dispose of her body. She survived with a fractured skull and broken bones.

That escapade in the ice cream parlor had its humorous overtones, but at its core it was a deadly encounter with a desperate man, a guy who abused a young woman and tried to kill her, and would kill a cop too if he got pressed. That sort of low-life is the kind you relish getting behind bars.

The victim orientation permeates a cop's approach to his work. It sets him aside from those who see only the offender several months later in court. It's why cops are uniformly turned off by the pleas for mercy for those found guilty under the law. The cops remember the victim.

One hears talk of "victimless" crimes, but I don't think there is such a thing. Dope, prostitution, gambling—all of these deposit their residue of destruction on others, even people far beyond the participants. The enormous cost of welfare payments, medical bills, and police time come out of the pockets of the taxpayers, who are also victims of "victimless" crime.

That may sound harsh and even unchristian. Yet I've never thought justice was unchristian. I've never thought being a

Christian was synonymous with being a pansy, or even a mild-mannered Clark Kent. Jesus grew up in a carpenter's home, so He probably wrestled logs and huge stacks of lumber. He was not afraid to drive the thieves from the Temple and exercise righteous judgment against them. (Luke 19:45-46)

The proper use of force did not cease to be a question as I climbed the ranks of police work. I began planning strategies which would put criminals behind bars with as little bloodshed as possible.

When I was promoted from captain to commander in the detective bureau, one of the first details I received was to address the rising number of gang related crimes.

There had been considerable gang activity in L.A. in the 1950's, but most of it was in the Mexican-American community. For some reason that activity tapered off during the 60's. Then it started with a flourish in the early 70's, especially among blacks.

Two gangs in particular would rove up and down the streets. When they saw somebody they wanted to shoot, they would start firing indiscriminately. Many times they would hit innocent people near them. Benjy, a gang member had been after someone in a rival gang. When he found him, he began firing wildly right in front of a homecoming float from one of the local high schools. Several of the beauty queens were shot. I sat in on the interrogation.

"Copper, I've got a name now, a reputation. I'm the Enforcer. There ain't nobody going to hassle me."

"If any of those girls who were on that float die, you're going to have more than a reputation, Benjy."

"Hey, man. That's even better. Besides, I'm a juvenile. I didn't know no better."

"Enough of that, Benjy. Why'd you do it?"

"I told you, man. It's my reputation. I'm a big man. I'm the Enforcer. If the gang wants somebody killed, I'm the one to do it."

"Are you willing to go to prison for three or four years just for a reputation?"

Benjy grinned at the other officer and me. "Man, I've been losing a little weight lately. My teeth are bad and I've got a dose of VD I need treated. Three or four years I come home healthy with my rep intact and graduated from the pen."

He grinned again and I left the room.

The public was incensed and demanded that the police make the streets secure again. My boss, Deputy Chief Pete Nelson, instructed me to get together with my counterpart in the patrol bureau who had been assigned the same areas. We were to come up with a gang task force and a plan of action. We did come up with a strategy.

Our objective was to arrest the hardcore leadership. This would include about fifteen percent of the gang's membership. Removing the leaders, we reasoned, would press the others into fewer violent crimes. For several months, we carefully executed the plan, concentrating specifically on nailing the leaders. Through a series of informants, we were also able to determine who was actually doing the shootings.

Just as we were seeing progress, three guys picked up by the gang squad escaped from juvenile hall and later stole some guns. Armed and dangerous, they vowed they would shoot it out with the police rather than allow themselves to be recaptured.

An informant told us the escapees were holed up in a housing project with two other leaders of their gang. They were quite vocal about shooting it out. They knew our reluctance to have a gun battle with under-age juveniles. We could imagine the public furor if the police killed several teenagers.

When I received the information on the gang members' location, I checked to verify it. When I was certain of their hideout, I said, "Let's hit them at three o'clock in the morning."

Because juveniles were involved, I decided to lead the unit personally. If a gun battle erupted, I wanted to be able to vouch for the attempts that were made to avoid it.

A dozen of us assembled at the housing project at 3 a.m. We were a little edgy because everyone knew we would have to undergo extra risks because of our commitment to see that no kids were shot. My instructions came close to saying, "Don't use your gun even if the other guy's pointing one at you." At the same time, I didn't want any of my men shot.

We were concerned about entry because the doors had steel frames. That made them too tough to kick in without losing the advantage of surprise. Fortunately, the director of the housing unit agreed to provide us with a key.

We slipped up the stairs and tried the key, fearing the lock might have been altered. The key worked. We slammed the door open and caught the guys still in bed. We were on them so quickly they didn't have a chance to get their guns. Not one shot was fired.

That incident was typical of the gang task force's operation and success. Because of its effectiveness, it became a prototype for the department under the acronym CRASH, Community Resources Against Street Hoodlums. CRASH continued as a highly successful deterrent to gang-related crime.

Over twenty years ago I was stopped short of my goal of becoming a pilot by a psychiatrist who took issue with my Christian beliefs. Years later, when I took the deputy chief's exam, my strong Christian witness was a decisive aid. The oral exam was a forty- five minute interrogation by leading members of the community. One of the questions they asked was, "Aren't you the guy who was captain out at Venice?"

"Yes."

"What did you do out there? How did you pull that off?"

I answered, "Well, I prayed a lot."

They laughed and thought I was joking.

"No, I really did. I don't want in any sense to play down the qualified staff I had. They gave me a lot of good ideas and I utilized them. They really were super and there are some practical things that I can describe that we did."

"But I literally prayed every day as I entered the Venice area. I had a pattern of praying. I would pray for my family from one major freeway turn-off to the next, and for friends from there to here. Then, when I crossed over to Venice until I arrived at the station, I asked God to give me the wisdom to do the right thing for the people. And He did."

"As I look back, He gave me a lot of ideas that shouldn't have occurred to a guy as young as I was. The ideas would come to me and in many cases they provided just the right strategy for a situation. I hadn't really thought of things in those terms. I have to say that wisdom was given to me."

They looked at me and one of them said, "You believe in a personal God?"

"Yes, I do."

We had a conversation about that and as time passed, one of them commented, "With the trends in government, maybe you're the type of guy we're after—someone who knows what he believes and who has firm convictions."

I received the highest overall score of all the candidates, even though I was probably the youngest. I was soon made one of the deputy chiefs of the Los Angeles Police Department. I honestly believe that God has put me here, for when I'm doing police work, I know that is what the Lord would have Bob Vernon do. Colossians 3:23 says, "Whatever you do, do your work heartily as for the Lord rather than for men." When I walk into my office each morning I do it saying, "This is the Lord's work." That means that every one of my decisions and actions as a manager and administrator is a sermon to my 2,000 men. My stance on discipline, my fairness, or lack of it, is a witness.

The struggle goes on. I still feel the pressures, still go through the tests. They may be a little different now, but the basic struggles in the life of a deputy chief are the same as in the life of a street cop. The beautiful part about being a Christian cop is that God goes with me. I have an additional dimension to my life—a spiritual one.

I'm not the only one. Hundreds of policemen I know have been "born again," too. Many of us get together at Hume Lake Christian Camp with our spouses for a police couples' conference. Interest is so high we've had to schedule two weekends each year with over three hundred attending each session. Most officers recognize a need for a special strength and direction in their lives. When they ask me how my relationship with God started, I tell them this story.

When I was deputy chief over personnel training I issued a notice that bulletproof vests were available. They had been tested at the academy and they really would stop bullets. They were constructed of a material similar to nylon, woven very tightly, a quarter of an inch thick and weighing less than four pounds.

Initially, only a handful of officers bought them. One of those who did was sitting at an intersection on his motorcycle when a pickup truck whipped through the stop sign. He cranked up and gave chase, thinking he had a citation.

It was early in the morning in the south part of L.A., the air was crisp and he still had his gloves on. As he approached the truck, he started casually removing his gloves, preparing to write a traffic citation.

He didn't know that the guy had just robbed a store and had the money and the gun on the seat alongside him. Of course, the bandit thought the cop had stopped him for the robbery.

The cop approached his window and said, "Morning, sir. May I see your driver's…" BLAM!

The bandit shot him point blank, about two feet from his chest. The impact of the bullet knocked him to the pavement. Then to the horror of the bandit, the cop pulled out his revolver and fired a shot into the cab. The guy threw out the gun and gave up.

That motorcycle cop didn't just believe in bulletproof vests, he had faith. He demonstrated the same truth that reached me as a young twelve-year-old attending a Good News Evangelism Class. The lady teaching made the point that not only do we have to believe that God wants to save us, we have to experience it by faith.

It's a point I've made to police officers time and again using the illustration of the bulletproof vest. "We can't look at the vest and say, 'I believe the vest will protect me from bullets.' Nor can we look at God and impersonally say, 'I believe that He's there.'"

"We have to put Him on. We have to invite Him into our life. We have to make it personal and take our beliefs to the point of commitment and action."

Police work *is* compatible with Christianity. The lessons I've learned from effective cops like Nick Najera—being friendly (even with the bad guys), using minimal force, being fair and honest, maintaining the ability to be compassionate, are biblical principles, and they work.

I've got to say that my personal relationship with God has worn well. He's given me the strength I've needed to meet the anger, frustration, fears and heartache I've experienced in fulfilling the demanding role of peacemaker in blue.

EPILOGUE

Assistant Chief Robert L. Vernon ended his career with the L.A.P.D. in June of 1992 after serving for nearly 38 years. The following year, an opportunity to travel throughout Europe under the auspices of the International Christian Business Men's Committee was offered to him. For two weeks he and his wife, Esther, visited six countries where Bob spoke about issues facing law enforcement in Los Angeles specifically, and in the United States in general. At each of the speaking venues he concluded with a presentation of the Gospel. God blessed the sessions and the results were rewarding.

From these meetings Bob made strategic contacts. Many of the countries were interested in having Bob return to provide in person leadership training to their police forces. God had prepared him for this new chapter of life in several ways. His educational accomplishments had given him an open door into teaching and his training in Government at the prestigious

Claremont Graduate School in California provided him additional structure for his lectures. More importantly, Bob and Esther sat under the teaching ministry of Pastor John MacArthur of Grace Community Church for 21 years and the Scriptures gave him the foundation for a biblically-based view of servant-leadership. He returned home from Europe with the task of developing a leadership seminar for law enforcement.

The following year Bob was lecturing in Europe. As the word spread about his new courses, other countries began asking him to train their law enforcement officers. Bob's speaking calendar quickly filled up and he soon realized that help was needed with all the opportunities that were becoming available to him. He began recruiting and training Christian officers with teaching abilities to meet the growing demand. A steady stream of officers from Christian police associations expressed their desire to participate in the same training and The Pointman Leadership Institute (PLI) was "born" with great enthusiasm.

The bedrock principles of PLI came from the Ten Commandments and were adapted using secular terminology. The organization has seen steady growth and its leadership training has expanded beyond international law enforcement agencies to include governments, businesses and churches. Currently, seventy-five countries have received Bob's training with over 100,000 police personnel served. Today, there are regional PLI directors in Africa, South America, Europe and the United States, with 70 instructors available to train throughout the world. Throughout PLI's 25 year history, at the end of every seminar, the teacher concludes with one optional session where they share their Christian testimonies and the Gospel is clearly presented. In most cases, all attendees returned to hear the presentation and in many cases they accept the invitation to receive salvation in Christ.

Bob Vernon used his gifts of storytelling in his early ministry with teenagers. He found that the stories kept their attention and helped them apply the spiritual truths he taught. Without realizing it, he was using the same teaching method that Jesus used as He taught parables. Many of Bob's stories came from his real-life experiences on the streets of Los Angeles—some of which are told in this book.

It is clear that Bob's career with the L.A.P.D. made it possible for him to fulfill his promise as a young man to serve his Lord. At that time his answer was, "Jesus, I'll do whatever You want me to do." It seemed unlikely that a police career could fulfill that call from the Lord and little did he know where that path would lead! As Bob looked back in amazement to see the many opportunities he was given to serve his Lord, he often said that he was just the kid who lived on Mosher Ave!

God's call is always one of obedience. Remember, God desires a willing heart!

Whatever you do, do it heartily, as to the Lord, and not to men.
Colossians 3:23

God's Plan of Salvation

Everyone is destined to die, but life does not end with death. The Bible says that after death there will be a judgment where each person will give an account of his life to God (Hebrews 9:27). When God created Adam and Eve in His own image in the garden of Eden, He gave them an abundant life, and the freedom to choose between good and evil. They chose to disobey God and go their own way. As a consequence, death was introduced into the human race, not only physical death, but also spiritual death. For this reason, all human beings are separated from God.

Unfortunately, man continues to disobey God: *for all have sinned and fall short of the glory of God (Romans 3:23).* This is humanity's problem: because of sin everyone is separated from God (Isaiah 59:2).

People have tried to overcome this separation in many ways: by doing good, through religion or philosophy, or by attempting to live morally and justly. However, none of these things is enough to cross the barrier of separation between God and humanity, because God is holy and human beings are sinful.

This spiritual separation has become the condition of mankind, and because of this they are condemned: *He who believes in Him is not judged; he who does not believe has been judged already, because he has not believed in the name of the only begotten Son of God (John 3:18).* There is only one solution to the problem: *Unless one is born again he cannot see the kingdom of God (John 3:3);* that is, it is necessary to be born again in the spiritual sense. God Himself has provided the means that makes it possible for anyone to be born again, and this is the plan that He has for us because He loves us.

God's Love and Plan

Jesus Christ said:

For God so loved the world that He gave His only begotten Son, that whoever believes in Him shall not perish, but have eternal life (John 3:16).

I came that they may have life, and have it abundantly (John 10:10). He who believes in the Son has eternal life; but he who does not obey the Son will not see life, but the wrath of God abides on him (John 3:36).

I am the way, and the truth, and the life; no one comes to the Father but through Me (John 14:6).

God's holiness makes it impossible for Him to relate to sinful humanity, and His justice demands that the sinner be judged and condemned to eternal separation from God. Because of this, man became the enemy of God. Although God has every right to condemn humanity, because of His love He provided a solution through His Son, Jesus, who bore the sins of humanity on the cross. Jesus' death was the only acceptable sacrifice for sin: *And there is salvation in no one else; for there is no other name under heaven that has been given among men by which we must be saved (Acts 4:12).*

When Jesus died on the cross, He died for us, thereby establishing a bridge that unites God and humanity. Because of this sacrifice, every person who is born again can have true fellowship with God.

Jesus Christ Is Alive Today

After Jesus Christ died on the cross at Calvary, where He received the punishment that we deserved, the Bible says that He was buried in a tomb. But He did not remain there:

He resurrected! For all those who believe in Jesus Christ, the resurrection is a guarantee that they will also be resurrected to eternal life in the presence of God. This is very good news! *Christ died for our sins...was buried, and...He was raised on the third day according to the Scriptures (1 Corinthians 15:3-4).*

How to Receive God's Love and Plan

In His mercy, God has determined that salvation is free. To receive it, agree with and believe these five things:

1. Acknowledge the problem (separation from God because of sin).

2. Admit to being a sinner, and that you need salvation.

3. Recognize that Jesus Christ died on the cross for your sins.

4. Commit yourself to Jesus Christ so that He can save and guide you.

5. Receive Jesus Christ as your personal Savior and Lord, now.

The Bible says:

that if you confess with your mouth Jesus as Lord, and believe in your heart that God raised Him from the dead, you will be saved (Romans 10:9).

For whoever will call on the name of the Lord will be saved (Romans 10:13).

A Prayer to Receive Jesus Christ

Lord Jesus, I know that I have sinned against You and that I do not live according to Your plan; therefore, I ask You to forgive me. I believe that You died for me, and in doing so, You paid the debt for my sins. I repent of my sin and now I want to live the kind of life that You want me to live. I ask you to come into my life and be my personal Savior. Help me to follow You and to obey You as Lord. Allow me to discover Your good and perfect will for my life.

Your Prayer. God's Promise.

When you pray to receive Jesus Christ as the Savior and Lord of your life, He hears you and several things take place: your sins are forgiven (Colossians 2:13), you become a child of God (John 1:12), and you receive eternal life (John 3:16).

You may feel strong emotions because of this decision, but do not let yourself be carried away, as your feelings can change from day to day. Don't put your confidence on the way you felt when you accepted Christ. Daily put your complete confidence for salvation in Jesus' work on the cross.

Fellowship with God daily through prayer and by reading His word, the Bible. Try to have fellowship with other Christians so that you can receive support and spiritual guidance.

The Promises of God are Fulfilled

He who has the Son has the life; he who does not have the Son of God does not have the life. These things I have written to you who believe in the name of the Son of God, so that you may know that you have eternal life (1 John 5:12-13). This is the beginning of the abundant life that Jesus Christ came to offer, because God desires to restore what was lost in the Garden of Eden. Now, you *will* be with Him in heaven!

CONNECT WITH US!

THREE
SIXTEEN
PUBLISHING

Sign up for announcements about new Bibles,
books and more.

316PUBLISHING.COM